FOCUS ON EDUCATION

Series Editor: Trevor Kerry

Teaching Science

A teaching skills workbook

M.K. Sands B.Sc., Ph.D., M.I.Biol..

University of Nottingham

R.A. Hull M.A., M.Inst.P.

University of Nottingham

Nelson

Thomas Nelson and Sons Ltd
Nelson House   Mayfield Road
Walton-on-Thames   Surrey
KT12 5PL   UK

51 York Place
Edinburgh
EH1 3JD   UK

Thomas Nelson (Hong Kong) Ltd
Toppan Building 10/F
22A Westlands Road
Quarry Bay   Hong Kong

Thomas Nelson Australia
102 Dodds Street
South Melbourne
Victoria 3205   Australia

Nelson Canada
1120 Birchmount Road
Scarborough   Ontario
M1K 5G4   Canada

© M K Sands, R A Hull 1985

First published by Macmillan Education Ltd 1985
ISBN 0-333-37821-0

This edition published by Thomas Nelson and Sons Ltd 1992

ISBN 0-17-448189-6
NPN 9 8 7 6 5 4 3

Printed in Hong Kong.

CONTENTS

ACKNOWLEDGEMENTS

The authors and publishers wish to thank the following who have kindly given permission for the use of copyright material:

The Association for Science Education for an extract from *Education through Science*, the 1981 Policy Statement of the Association;

The Controller of Her Majesty's Stationery Office for tables from *Science in Schools*, Assessment of Performance Unit, Report No. 1 1982;

Dr Paul Gardner for an extract from his *Words in Science* report (1972);

The Institute of Physics for a table from *Girls and Physics*.

The titles in this series are designed to examine basic teaching skills in their respective subject areas. Each title is laid out as a workbook so that the practitioner can utilise his or her own classroom as a basis for progressive professional self-development.

Impetus for the series came out of the DES-financed Teacher Education Project, which ran from 1976 to 1980 in the Universities of Nottingham, Leicester and Exeter. That project explored general teaching skills: class management, questioning, explaining and the handling of mixed ability classes and of exceptional pupils. A direct outcome from the work of the Teacher Education Project was a series of skills workbooks under the general title *Focus*, which was published through the years 1981 and 1982.

It is, perhaps, a measure of the success of the *Focus* series that I was approached by a number of colleagues in the universities involved, with the proposal for a Curriculum series of workbooks which would apply some of the teaching skills highlighted and researched by the project to specific subject areas.

Each title in the current curriculum series is aimed at subject teachers in the appropriate field. Our corporate intention is to make each workbook immediately relevant to the needs of three main groups of users: qualified teachers of the subject in question; teachers qualified in some other discipline who find themselves pressed into service on less familiar ground; and students in training in the subject area concerned. Past experience has led us to believe that each exercise is adaptable for use at various levels of sophistication according to the stage reached by the user and to his or her own needs.

Each workbook has a tripartite format. Part 1 is intended to start the user thinking about issues in the particular curriculum area, and many of the activities designed for this purpose can be carried out away from the classroom itself. In Part 2 a collection of practical exercises encourages teachers to become more self-aware and to scrutinise their own practice. A final section helps the teachers reflect on practice and experience by relating classroom events to research and theory. Within this basic structure individual authors are given some flexibility to interpret their own theme.

The series makes frequent demands on teachers to get together in order to watch one another at work: a process we have labelled 'observational pairing'. Traditionally the classroom has been 'a fine and private place' as Marvell might have put it. We believe that professional self-respect demands that a more open attitude should prevail.

It is especially opportune to be producing the curriculum series of workbooks at a time when economic stringencies are making in-roads into the education service in general and into in-service provision in particular. There is a mounting public pressure for increased accountability by the teaching profession. This series will, we believe, help to make teachers more analytical in their teaching and more articulate in expressing the rationale for their work. It will also fill a void for really practical advice for all those whose jobs involve a responsibility for professional training, as university and college tutors, inspectors, advisers, teachers' centre wardens, headteachers and heads of subject departments.

Dr Trevor Kerry
*Doncaster Metropolitan Institute
of Higher Education*

INTRODUCTION

This workbook is designed to help you teach science. It contains a series of activities which focus on practical teaching skills, and on important issues in science teaching and how these are interpreted in the classroom. BEd or PGCE students on teacher training courses will be able to use the material in the book under the guidance of their tutors. Qualified teachers may welcome the chance to practise specific skills, alone or with their colleagues. A workbook such as this can easily be adapted to form part of an in-service training course, and can be used by a science department as part of a programme of professional development. In some of the exercises it is suggested that an observer should watch and comment on the performance of the skills being practised. Some teachers, particularly those who have not worked in schools which are open-plan, nor in team-teaching situations, may find the idea of being observed a little daunting. However, the amount to be learned by the pooling of ideas between professionals is well worth the apprehension generated by these 'observational pairing' lessons. Teachers have a lot to learn from each other, and the exercises here will yield more if they are talked over with colleagues.

This science teaching workbook is one of a series concerned with the skills of teaching. Much of the material has been subjected in trial form to scrutiny by individual students and teachers, and by tutors and advisers responsible for planning and implementing courses. It is flexible in the options it leaves open for the user to construct his or her own way of working with the material and to adapt the ideas and activities to particular circumstances. It is not intended to be a definitive statement of how science should be taught nor an exhaustive summary of all the skills required in a competent science teacher. Nonetheless, a teacher using the material efficiently will be able to improve many aspects of his or her teaching.

We acknowledge the help of Florence Davies who wrote the material for Part 1, Topic 5 (*Study strategies for science texts*).

Part 1

PREPARING TO TEACH SCIENCE

Topic 1
WHY TEACH SCIENCE?

Answers to the question 'Why teach science?' are often concerned with three approaches to the subject. These are:

> Science has intrinsic value as a body of accumulated knowledge and as a way of finding out about the world.

> Learning science is a means for helping individuals to fulfil their own personal potential.

> Learning science helps the individual to learn to live in a society and both to contribute to it and to benefit from it.

There is pressure to broaden the basis of science teaching, because it is felt that we have perhaps been too concerned with the first of these approaches, particularly with science as a body of knowledge, at the expense of the other two.

It is often found to be convenient for practical purposes to make a distinction between the *aims or goals* and the *objectives* of science education. Aims or goals are broad statements of principle. For example, the Association for Science Education in its 1981 policy statement lists the following aims:

> The acquisition of a knowledge and understanding of a range of scientific concepts, generalizations, principles and laws through the systematic study and experience of aspects of the body of knowledge called science.

> The acquisition of a range of cognitive and psycho-motor skills and processes as a result of direct involvement in scientific activities and procedures in the laboratory and the field.

> The utilization of scientific knowledge and processes in the pursuit of further knowledge and deeper understanding, and the development of an ability to function autonomously in an area of science studies to solve practical problems and to communicate that experience to others.

> The attainment of a perspective or way of looking at the world together with some understanding of how it complements and contrasts with other perspectives or ways of organizing knowledge and inquiry.

> The attainment of a basic understanding of the nature of advanced technological societies, the interaction between science and society, and the contribution science makes to our cultural heritage.

> The realization that scientific knowledge and experience is of some value in the process of establishing a sense of personal and social identity.
>
> *Association for Science Education*, 1981, p. 11.

Aims or goals tend to be rather general statements, difficult to translate directly into what to do with 3X on a wet Friday afternoon. Objectives are statements which are sufficiently specific for a science teacher to be able to translate them into action. They are likely to be sharper in meaning if they have:

> a *verb* which specifies an activity

> an *object of the verb* which indicates clearly and definitely what the verb applies to.

Compare, for example, the specific objective 'interpreting data presented in tabular or graphical form' with the more vaguely formulated objective 'understanding scientific data'.

Because of the widespread use of aims and objectives in curricula and examinations, it behoves a teacher to understand both, and to see how they can be translated into teaching and learning activities. Activities 1 and 2 below are aimed at helping you to review your own aims and how you put them into practice.

Activity 1:
Reviewing the aims of
science teaching

The aims listed in Table 1 emphasise some of the general educational purposes of science teaching.

1 Indicate how important you think each aim is by ringing the appropriate number.
2 Select a science topic which you have recently taught or discussed. Think what teaching and learning activities you might use to develop the aims which you considered important in 1. (For example, the study of waste materials would probably not be a conventional science activity to include in a topic on materials, but could help to achieve a number of the aims, in particular (a), (b), (e), (g), (h), (j), (k), (l), (m).)

TABLE 1: THE AIMS OF SCIENCE TEACHING

Aim	Very important			Unimportant	TOPIC: How to develop the aim in this topic
(a) To develop knowledge and awareness of the natural environment	4	3	2	1	
(b) To develop knowledge and awareness of the man-made environment	4	3	2	1	
(c) To develop knowledge and awareness of the applications of science in the home	4	3	2	1	
(d) To develop understanding and awareness of the importance of technology	4	3	2	1	
(e) To develop interest in and knowledge of the local environment (natural, man-made, including local industry)	4	3	2	1	
(f) To encourage and develop actual or potential leisure activities	4	3	2	1	

Aim	Very important		Unimportant		TOPIC: How to develop the aim in this topic
(g) To develop good attitudes to science (e.g. realise potential for good as well as dangers for evil, need for social responsibility of scientists)	4	3	2	1	
(h) To develop scientific attitudes (e.g. inquiring mind, critical attitude, honesty, caution in making claims, being methodical and careful)	4	3	2	1	
(i) To develop practical skills	4	3	2	1	
(j) To help to develop mathematical skills	4	3	2	1	
(k) To develop logical thinking skills	4	3	2	1	
(l) To develop problem-solving skills	4	3	2	1	
(m) To help to develop pupils' skills in English	4	3	2	1	

Activity 2:
Reviewing the aims of practical work in the 11-13 age range

In a survey of practical work by Beatty and Woolnough (1982) it was found that most teachers estimated that, with the 11-13 age range, between 40 and 80% of class time was spent on practical work. It is therefore important that the aims of practical work at this level should be clear. The aims which Beatty and Woolnough presented to teachers in a questionnaire are listed in Table 2. In the first column put the aims in what you think is their order of importance. In the second column enter the order in which the teachers themselves put these aims, given upside-down below the table. Then comment on the similarities and differences between the two orders. Compare your own order with that of colleagues. A blank column is included so that you can also record your attitudes at a later date.

TABLE 2: AIMS OF PRACTICAL WORK IN THE 11-13 AGE RANGE

	YOUR ORDER	TEACHERS' ORDER
1 As a creative activity		
2 For finding facts and arriving at new principles		
3 To arouse and maintain interest		
4 To be able to comprehend and carry out instructions		
5 To develop a critical attitude		

6 To develop an ability to communicate

7 To develop an ability to cooperate

8 To develop certain disciplined attitudes

9 To develop self-reliance

10 To develop specific manipulative skills

11 To elucidate theoretical work as an aid to comprehension

12 To encourage accurate observation and description

13 To give experience in standard techniques

14 To help remember facts and principles

15 To indicate the industrial aspects of science

16 To make phenomena more real through experience

17 To practise seeing problems and seeking ways to solve them

18 To prepare the student for practical examinations

19 To promote a logical reasoning method of thought

20 To verify facts and principles already taught

Comments

Aim	Order	Aim	Order	Aim	Order	Aim	Order
1	16	6	8	11	17	16	4
2	11	7	13	12	1	17	9
3	2	8	7	13	15	18	20
4	5	9	14	14	10	19	3
5	12	10	9	15	19	20	18

For Further Study

Association for Science Education, 'Education Through Science', *School Science Review*, 1981, **63**, 222

Beatty, J.W. and Woolnough, B.E., 'Why do practical work in 11-13 science?' *School Science Review*, 1982, **63**, 225, p. 768

Richardson, M. and Boyle, C., *What is Science?*, Association for Science Education (Study Series No. 15), 1979

Topic 2
CLASS MANAGEMENT,
CONTROL AND SAFETY

Management and control probably cause more concern to new teachers than any other aspect of teaching. They will be given the same basic advice by almost everyone:

- Be more firm at the start than you mean to be in the end.
- Ensure that lessons are well-planned and have a clear structure; good control and effective management are then less of a problem.

It is most important to:

- give the pupils work which is *appropriate* to their age and ability
- provide *variety* in lessons (in activity, teaching technique, content)
- develop the art of *pacing* activities to fit the available time.

Activities 3 and 4 develop these points and help you to think through some class management situations.

Activity 3:
Assessing your class
management and control

Table 3 contains practical advice for science teachers on class management and control. It is organised into things to do at various points before, during, and after the lesson. Find an opportunity to use it as a checklist, both for yourself and for an observer of your lesson. Allow yourself and the observer a few minutes after the lesson to complete a copy of the list. Be honest with yourself, for you are then likely to be able to accept more easily any critical points raised by the observer when he or she discusses the lesson with you.

TABLE 3: A CLASS MANAGEMENT CHECKLIST

DATE:	CLASS:	TIME:
Course of action	*Yes/No*	*Comment*

Before

1 Prepare lesson thoroughly and give it a clear structure

2 Book apparatus well in advance with a written list of what is required

3 Prepare furniture and apparatus in the room before pupils arrive (if possible)

4 Practise experiments before the lesson

5 Know how many of each item of apparatus you have at the start

6 Plan distribution and collection of apparatus

7 Have extra material available for able and weak pupils

8 Arrive at the room before the pupils

Start

9 Control the pupils' entry into the room

10 Get silence and attention before you start speaking

11 Start the lesson 'with a bang', clearly and definitely

12 Deal with latecomers quickly and efficiently

During

13 Know and use pupils' names

14 Give clear instructions

15 Organise transitions between activities carefully

16 Be mobile: walk round, don't 'hide' behind the front bench

17 Look at the class when speaking and scan the pupils

18 Get feedback frequently by asking questions

19 Spread questions around the class and involve pupils

20 Clarify and insist on *your* standards

21 Anticipate discipline problems; act quickly if
they arise

22 Avoid full-scale confrontations which you cannot
win

23 Be firm and consistent in giving punishments

24 Don't patronise pupils, treat them as responsible
beings

25 Use praise and encouragement to increase motivation

26 Show yourself as a helper and facilitator to
the pupils

27 Insist on safe procedures

End

28 Allow time to pack up and clear away before the bell

29 Count items of equipment back

30 Look round before pupils go to make sure room
is tidy

31 Quieten class before dismissal and insist it is orderly

After

32 Record in your lesson notes any mistakes you made

33 Suggest (after discussion, preferably) five points for
improvement

Activity 4:
Coping with management problems

Consider each of the four situations given in the text below. In each case, identify the potential management problems, and suggest what action you might take to avoid or minimise them. Discuss your suggestions with colleagues. Afterwards, discuss any awkward situations from your own experience which, by forethought, could have been prevented or minimised in their effect.

1 A first-year class undertaking a practical lesson involving heating water in beakers using bunsen burners, all the apparatus being stored in the laboratory.

POTENTIAL PROBLEM

E.g. collection of apparatus

POSSIBLE ACTION

Collect one bench at a time.
Teacher/technician could spread material around lab in advance.

2 Pupils in a second-year class looking at the magnetic field lines of small magnets with plotting compasses and iron filings.

POTENTIAL PROBLEM

E.g. magnets become covered with iron filings which are difficult to remove

POSSIBLE ACTION

Keep the magnets in small polythene bags.

3 Pupils in a third-year class are to carry out a dissection of a bull's eye.

POTENTIAL PROBLEM	POSSIBLE ACTION
E.g. some pupils refuse to carry out the dissection.	Have alternative work available.

4 Pupils are to use a circus of different experiments in a lesson.

POTENTIAL PROBLEM	POSSIBLE ACTION
E.g. experiments vary in length	Plan activities involving writing to act as buffers

Experienced science teachers make many management and control decisions in every lesson with an ease which a novice can only envy. One of the reasons is that they have probably experienced similar events many times before. To give you some practice in this type of decision-making a few common situations are given below. Discuss them and try to decide what you would do if something similar occurred to you. Some questions to ask yourself are:

- Have I got enough *information*? If not, how might I get it?
- What might be the *cause*?
- What *options* are there available?
- What *reasoning* can I apply when choosing one of these options? (E.g. effect on individual pupil, whole class; time taken to put into practice)
- What is my decision and why?

If you lack information, there is something to be said for a conservative strategy which prevents a problem from developing further, and allows time for the collection of information and more thought.

1 A pupil comes in five minutes after the lesson has started and goes straight to a seat at the back of the class, saying nothing to you?

2 In a practical lesson you thought you had set up equal size groups, but after five minutes they are of sizes 6, 4, 3, 3, 3, 3, 3, 1, 1?

3 Three pupils have written identical and very brief homework exercises?

4 A piece of apparatus is missing when you collect equipment after practical work?

Safety is clearly a very important matter in science, and all science teachers have to be continually aware of safety hazards. However, it should not be thought that school laboratories are particularly dangerous places. Only about 5 per cent of reported pupil accidents in school occur in laboratories; very few of the accidents are serious, and the number of children involved is something like 0.05 per cent. But this situation can only be maintained or improved upon if all science teachers have both a good knowledge of safety and the right attitude to it.

It is important that before teachers go into science lessons they know what the potential hazards are and take steps to minimise them, *and that they know what to do if an accident should occur in spite of their precautions.* They therefore need suitable reference materials. In the authors' opinion, the most useful material is the set of Hazcards produced by CLEAPSE (see **For Further Study**). These cards provide a reference index for safety hazards. It is also important for teachers to have a good general knowledge of safety and safety procedures, in the light of which the information on the Hazcards can be interpreted. The current edition of the Department of Education and Science booklet *Safety in Science Laboratories* is a good starting point for this, and is essential reading for anyone entering science teaching.

It is not possible to go into a lot of detail here about the complex issues which can arise in connection with safety. The material in Activities 6 and 7 and in Table 4 gives you some information on the most common accidents in laboratories, and poses some questions for you to consider.

Activity 6:
Reviewing common
types of accident

Table 4 gives categories of accident in school science laboratories. Put them in what you think is the correct order of frequency, and estimate what percentage each is of the total. The order and frequency as established in a survey are given upside-down beneath the table. Compare these with your own estimates.

TABLE 4: COMMON TYPES OF ACCIDENT IN SCIENCE LABORATORIES

CATEGORY (alphabetical order)	YOUR ESTIMATE (Number and %)	SURVEY RESULT %
(a) Animal bites		
(b) Burns, caused by flames, hot objects, scalds		
(c) Chemicals in the eyes		
(d) Chemicals in the mouth		
(e) Chemicals on the body (not eyes, mouth)		
(f) Cuts		
(g) Dropping, falling, slipping, knocking, lifting		
(h) Electric shock		
(i) Explosions		
(j) Fainting		
(k) Inhalation		

Order: 1(c) 22.8% 2(e) 20.6% 3(f) 20.3% 4(b) 14.5% 5(g) 7.3% 6(d) 4.1% 7(k) 3.7% 8(a) 2.8% 9(i)(j) 1.5%, 1.5% 11(h) 0.6%

Source: Tawney, D. 'Accidents in School Laboratories: A Report of an Investigation', *Education in Science*, Nov. 1981, 95, p. 32.

Activity 7: Looking at safety reference material

Use the following questions to help you learn to find your way around the reference literature which is available to you on safety.
 (i) How do you cut glass tubing safely?
 (ii) How do you get glass tubing through a hole in a rubber bung safely?
 (iii) 'Please sir, is copper sulphate poisonous?' 'Yes, why?' 'I've just drunk some sir.' What should you do? (This happened to one of the authors.)
 (iv) How would you get rid of a small quantity of bromine?
 (v) The taking of small quantities of blood from pupils in science lessons is potentially very hazardous and should not be undertaken by student teachers unless they are fully supervised by a specialist biology teacher and know very clearly that they are adopting correct procedures. Why is it potentially hazardous? What are the correct procedures? (See, for example, *Education in Science*, April 1979, p. 27.)
 (vi) The situation described below is extremely dangerous. Why? What is correct procedure?
 A student teacher is wrestling with the valve of the gas cylinder which is propped loosely against a wall. 'This . . . . . valve is stuck,' he says, 'Let's get a hammer to it.'

For Further Study

ASE, *Topics in Safety* (1982)

Bishop, A.J. and Whitfield, R.C., *Situations in Teaching*, McGraw-Hill, 1972. This book gives a large number of both general and scientific situations to think about. A short introduction discusses some of the issues of decision-making.

CLEAPSE Development Group, CLEAPSE Hazcards (plus 1981 supplement); available from Association for Science Education

DES, *Safety in Science Laboratories* (Safety series No. 2), HMSO (use current edition)

Wragg, E.C., *Class Management and Control*, Focus Books, Macmillan, 1981

**Topic 3
COMPOSING
WORKSHEETS**

You are proposing to use a worksheet with a class. How can your worksheet help you to get the pupils to do what you want them to do? Before you start writing, read the guidelines which follow.

Put your selected activities into a suitable order. Check these activities carefully to see that there will be variety as pupils work through them and that you have catered for the whole range of ability in the class. Are you clear about which are the core activities and which are the extension or additional activities for early finishers? Use this checklist to consider the layout and approach of the worksheet:

WORKSHEET CHECKLIST

Headings Use headings and sub-headings to organise the material and make it easier to read.

Summaries A summary at the start ('advance organiser') or at the end can be helpful to the learner.

Vocabulary Here you have to keep a balance between making it sufficiently straightforward for the pupils and fulfilling your role in the context of 'every teacher a teacher of English':

- try to avoid using formal language which is remote from the pupils' everyday usage (e.g. 'The remainder should be placed in a suitable container')

- consider whether scientific terms should be introduced, and if you do, highlight them by using capitals or underlining or in some other way

- avoid, or take particular care with words with double meanings or which have different meanings in science lessons from those found in general usage (e.g. energy, stomach)

- avoid abbreviations

Sentences Sentences are easier if they are short, contain few subordinate clauses, are written in the active form.

Experimental instructions Put instructions in the order in which the pupil needs to carry them out, giving advance warnings where necessary ('You will need ——— soon'). Explain how results are to be presented, before the practical activity, so that the required table can be drawn up in rough. Be precise ('one spatula' not 'a small amount'). Use questions to draw attention to important features. Give only one instruction at a time. At the start give a complete list of the apparatus the pupil needs. **Safety: Give clear warnings of precautions to be taken, and make sure they will be read before the practical work begins.**

Questions Make questions stand out. Word them directly and unambiguously. Make sure that it is clear to the pupils how and where to answer (e.g. a paragraph in an exercise book). Think about including questions which

- check comprehension: e.g. why did you heat the solution before ...?

- draw attention to important events: e.g. what happened when . . .?

- ask for interpretation: e.g. why do you think the blue colour . . .?

- ask for extrapolation: e.g. what do you think would have happened if . . .?

Diagrams In general, try to keep diagrams fairly simple. Label clearly where required. Make use of colour where appropriate. Flow diagrams can be useful, particularly for younger and less able pupils. Your diagrams should show the type of apparatus the class will be using, and not something slightly different in appearance.

Graphs and tables Remember to give titles and to label axes or categories clearly. Don't forget the units.

Layout Plan the layout before producing the final version. Use a grid to lay the work out neatly.

Make sure sections with different functions are clearly differentiated and try to fit the layout to the functions. Number each sub-heading and each page.

Write neatly or type to avoid having to spell out undecipherable handwriting. Good handwriting is better than bad typing, but make sure your writing is of a suitable size and style. CAPITALS are not as easy to read as words in lower case.

 Try to make *important* points stand out in some way, like the arrow used in the margin here.

Make it look attractive: would *you* want to pick it up and read it?

Pre-test Finally, think through the use of your worksheet. If you foresee any problems of organisation or safety, rewrite the relevant sections.
Before you make copies, try it out on one or two pupils.

Activity 8:
Writing and evaluating
a worksheet

1 Produce a worksheet for a first- or second-year science class, using the guidelines given in the text above.
2 Use your worksheet with a class.
3 After evaluating its use in the lesson and marking any response to it, go through these points:

Activities:
Was the order of activities right? An interesting exercise is to cut the worksheet into separate instructions, shuffle, and see if the same or a clearer order emerges when a colleague puts it back together.

If you incorporated activities for different levels of ability, were they successful in achieving your aims?

Were the activities interesting to the pupils and was the work worthwhile, relevant, useful?

Clarity:
Was the worksheet clear to everyone? How many questions for clarification did you get during the lesson?

Did any pupil answers show that your questions were ambiguous, badly phrased or at the wrong level?

Did any common responses suggest the need for further teaching of particular points?

Timing:
Did you allow the right amount of time for the work?

How did you keep the slower ones moving through the worksheet, so as not to have a drawn-out ending?

Was there time when all had finished to go over the work?

Include your worksheet and a summary of your evaluation in this book.

For Further Study

Collect a sample of worksheets from whatever sources are available to you. Use the checklist to evaluate them. Incorporate new ideas into your own repertoire.

Foster, D., *Resource-based Learning in Science*, Association for Science Education Study Series, No. 14, 1979

Green, E.L. (ed.), *Towards Independent Learning in Science*, Hart-Davis Educational, 1976

Misselbrook, H. (ed.), *Nuffield Secondary Science Teachers' Guide*, Longman, 1971

**Topic 4
MARKING PUPILS'
WORK IN SCIENCE**

Checking books and marking is an important and ever-present part of a teacher's job. Books are checked for a number of reasons. Some are:

- to correct the mistakes made by pupils
- to get them to carry out some remedial action
- to motivate them and make them work harder
- to find out where they have put their effort
- to encourage them
- to continue to inform the teacher, and also the pupil, of the pupil's progress
- to gain feedback on the effectiveness of the teaching.

Marks may be given to reward pupils, to enable comparisons between pupils, and for use by the school, parents and prospective employers. They may be given for attainment or effort.

It is not always easy to check pupils' written work as thoroughly and as well as one would wish. There is much marking to do, and time is always short, so planning ahead is needed to get work in from the pupils when you have time to mark and return it quickly. Perhaps more important is to mark the work effectively, so that the time spent on it has the maximum benefit. Beware, for example, of the two extremes: of covering the work in red ink which immediately alarms and depresses the recipient; or of giving no indication that you have actually read it, except for the final grade.

**Activity 9:
Marking**

Two answers to the same homework are given, both by 12-year-old pupils from a mixed ability class.

<u>15th Feb</u>

Prevention of heat loss

<u>Aim</u> To see if several thin layers keeps a person warmer than one thick layer.

<u>Diagram</u>

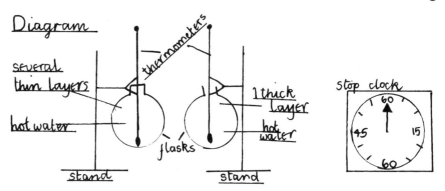

<u>Method</u> We set up the apparatus as shown in the diagram. We poured very hot water into the two flasks and took the temperature. We carried on taking the temperature every two mins for twenty mins. We held the flasks with stands and clamps because they werenot very safe on the bench.

<u>Results</u>

Time in mins	TEMPERATURE (°C)	
	several thin layers	1 thick layer
0	89	90
2	86	88
4	83	86
6	84	83
8	84	81
10	83	78
12	83	77
14	82	75
16	82	73
18	81	72
20	80	70

<u>Conclusion</u>

This experiment shows that several thin layers keep a person warmer than one thick layer.

Thin layers of clothing are better because they trap the air. This keeps the heat in because air is a bad conductor of heat. This is why explorers are advised to wear several layers of clothing in the arctic.

Aim To see if thick layers are better than a thin one

Put thE apartus as shown in the Diggram we use a flash with some thin stuff and a flast with one thick and take the tempretcher every to mirasfor 20 mins. We put a thromometer in the water weput q hiet hot water in the flash.

Results

thick one	thine one
90	89
88	86
86	83
83	83
81	84
80	84
78	84
77	83
	83

Con Cunsion

This is a concunsion to see which of the thin or thick coled down after the tempretcher ever 2 mins. Theis layers will kep a aninmal warm, thin tap the cold.

Mark the two pieces of work out of 10 and compare your marks with those given by others. Use these questions to aid your comparison:

... What variation is there in the marks given? Why?
... What was each person looking for in the work?
... What comments did you put on the work, and why?
... What do you think is the optimum number of comments you can make on a piece of work for maximum effect?
... How would you discuss the work and your comments with the pupil later?
... What does the work tell you about the pupil?
... What would you have told the class beforehand, about tackling the work set?

Besides set homework, pupils will also be doing other work such as making notes, writing records of practical work and drawing diagrams. How often should this be looked at, checked and/or marked? You are unlikely to have the time to mark each pupil's book comprehensively each week. Perhaps one week you may check for spelling and punctuation. Another time, you may choose an overall impression mark and comment. Make sure you know what you are looking for: presentation, tidiness, completeness, effort? Consider how you would convey these criteria to pupils.

Activity 10:
Making the maximum use
of marking time

Set some homework based on one of your lessons. Collect and mark the work. Return it to the class. Check the following points:

. . . Did you think out the kind of answer you wanted, decide on a mark scheme and/or decide how your marks would be given before you set the work?

. . . Did you explain to the class how you would be marking?

. . . Did handwriting and presentation have too great an effect on you? Were you lulled by a tidy page and neat writing into thinking an answer was a work of substance?

. . . Was the mark given with due consideration and not based on trivial points?

. . . Did you return the work as quickly as possible?

. . . Before or just after you returned the work did you say something nice about it, possibly mention praiseworthy efforts by name?

. . . Did you then go on to pick out the common errors, but without wasting everyone's time by going over all the mistakes?

. . . Did you talk to particular pupils individually where necessary?

. . . Did you remember that a pupil's belief in himself or herself can be strengthened or destroyed by the way you consistently respond to his work? Did you therefore check for the debilitating effect of constant criticism and low marks on the interest and effort of particular individuals?

. . . Did you keep a record of the marks, and a note of those who did not give their books in for follow-up?

Write below the title of the work set, the details of the marking scheme, and a list of points which arose from the marking, for discussion with the class.

Work set:

Marking scheme:

Points for discussion:

For Further Study

Read chapter 1 in Sutton, C. (ed.), *Communicating in the Classroom*, Hodder and Stoughton, 1981.

26

Topic 5
STUDY STRATEGIES
FOR SCIENCE TEXTS

This topic is concerned with ways in which pupils can be helped to learn effectively from written material in science. The term 'text' in the title refers not just to a textbook, but to any written material used in your teaching. The phrase 'science text' thus includes teacher-produced and commercial material and refers to passages from textbooks, extracts from reference books, notes given by the teacher or produced by the pupil, or any other literature used. Pupils have to be shown how to use this material effectively, and the summary in Table 5 suggests a number of study strategies which give support and direction for pupil learning from science texts. The strategies help in improving a pupil's reading ability, as the pupil has to read the text carefully in order to carry out the task set.

Activity 11:
Examining study
strategies

Table 5 outlines six study strategies which a teacher can organise using written material selected with the particular pupils in mind.
1 Read the table and consider, for your own subject and without referring to books, where each suggested strategy might be used.
2 For each of the six, note down one idea, stating the topic and the age group.

TABLE 5: STUDY STRATEGIES

Study strategy	What teacher does	What pupils do, individually or working in small groups	Follow-up
1 Marking information targets	(a) Selects or writes a passage relating to the class's current work. (b) Describes what it is that the the pupils are to search for in the text: maybe parts of a structure and their function (e.g. eye, barometer) or the sequence of actions in a process (e.g. water cycle, making a chemical substance). (c) Provides copies of the passage and instructions for pupils.	Search the text for the required information. Discuss and reach agreement on what it is. Underline the information in the text, and label it if necessary.	Pool results between groups and discuss with teacher. Possibly summarise the information in one of the diagrammatic forms described on page 28.
2 Summarising information in a table	(a) Selects or writes a passage from which information can be summarised or classified in a table (e.g. names, shape and function of different types of teeth). (b) Works out a suitable table shape and size to summarise the information. Fills in some table headings, the number depending on the ability of the class. (c) Provides copies of text or table outline for pupils and gives instructions on how to complete the table.	Find the required information by reading the text, and use it to complete (or construct) the summary table.	Pool results between groups and discuss with teacher. Reach agreement on suitable headings, and the completion of the rest of the table.

3 Summarising information in diagrammatic form	(a) Selects a diagram relating to the class's current work e.g. erupting volcano, lungs, thermometer. (b) Removes some or all labels from the diagram. (c) Gives pupils copies of the diagram and accompanying text from which the diagram is to be labelled.	Use the text to complete the labelling of the diagram.	Groups agree with teacher on the correct labels.
4 Summarising information in a flow chart	(a) Selects or writes a passage containing a procedure or process, e.g. instructions for practical work, the movements associated with breathing, feeding relationships of animals in a pond. (b) Constructs a flow chart, and fills in some steps or stages in selected boxes, leaving empty those where there is enough information in the text for pupils to complete. (c) Provides copies and instructions for pupils.	Locate, number and label steps or stages in the text before seeing the flow chart. Use the text to complete (or construct) the flow chart. Amplify and annotate the flow chart using the remaining information in the text.	Pool results between groups and discuss with teacher to reach agreement on the best way of presenting the information as a flow chart.
5 Ordering or sequencing information	(a) Selects a passage which gives a sequence, e.g. stages in digestion, explanation for sea breezes. (b) Rewrites text in sections corresponding to each stage. Cuts the text into these sections, shuffles (mounts on card for durability). (c) Provides copies and instructions for pupils.	Each group has a complete set of all the sections. They read it. Put them into what is thought to be the correct order.	Discuss final version and agree on best order. This need not be the same as the original. Useful before an experiment which is thus rehearsed before doing it.
6 Completing a text: cloze technique	(a) Selects a passage to be used in teaching or revision. (b) Rewrites passage with every fifth, seventh, ninth or twelfth word deleted, depending on the difficulty level of the passage and the ability of the class. (c) Provides copies and instructions for pupils.	Pupils read passage, consider and discuss possible words for the spaces. After agreement, complete the passage.	Teacher considers with class all suggestions for each space in the passage, asks groups to justify their choice as appropriate.
Your ideas:	1 2 3 4 5 6		

The study strategies described in Table 5 can be used for individual study. They are more effective if:

    ... each pupil has a copy of the text or passage being used which may be written on.

    ... pupils work in twos or threes on the task given.

    ... pupils in their groups are encouraged to discuss ideas and to collaborate in analysing the text. The objective is to use the text as scientific data and allow continuous feedback between pupils as they work on it.

Activity 12:
Using study strategies
effectively

Select the text you are going to use with a class and decide what you want pupils to focus on. It should, of course, be related to the work you are doing with the class. Select one of the study strategies to use with the text.

Make copies of the text you are going to use, and prepare any other material.

Plan the lesson procedure. This should include:
1 Distribution of materials
2 Giving the introduction
3 Monitoring and checking pupil work
4 Discussions with groups
5 Drawing the class together to allow the groups to contribute to the following discussion.

If possible, arrange to do one text-study lesson with each year group.

Evaluate the lesson: Make a note of the parts of the text which pupils found difficult, the alternative explanations which came up, and the way you would modify instructions or procedures in future.

For Further Study

Carré, C., *Language teaching and learning: Science*, Ward Lock Educational, 1981.

Davies, F. and Green, T., *Reading for Learning in Science*, Oliver and Boyd for the Schools Council, 1984.

Lunzer, E.A. and Gardner, K., *The Effective Use of Reading*, Heinemann, 1979.

Topic 6
OBSERVING SCIENCE TEACHING

Activity 13 is designed to help you learn through observation. It will be particularly helpful to teachers on their first visit to a school. It assumes that you will not be taking classes yourself, and that you will be able to observe lessons.

Activity 13:
Observing the science teacher's day

Arrange to spend a whole day with a teacher, attending and observing all the lessons he or she teaches during that day.

While you are observing the lessons, attempt the following exercises as seems appropriate. The first section is designed to structure your observation so that you become aware of teaching in terms of activities (both of the teacher and the class) rather than in terms of content only. The second asks you to look in particular at the management skills used in the lesson.

A *Teacher and pupil activities*
Throughout the day, keep a diary showing the variety and extent of the teacher's work during one day. Ask what further schoolwork (marking, lesson preparation, reading, administrative jobs, etc.) will be done during the evening. While you observe one lesson, list the ACTIVITIES which occur, using the following observation schedule.

Class	No. of pupils	Topic
Time	Teacher Activity	Pupil Activity

B *Lesson management*
During the day, select one lesson and watch specifically for the MANAGEMENT SKILLS used by the teacher. Use these headings which will later remind you of points in a lesson to which thought must be given beforehand in the planning. Discuss with the teacher any variation of approach with different classes.

MANAGEMENT SKILLS	YOUR COMMENTS
Starting the lesson (a) Entry to lab or classroom (b) Settling the class (c) Gaining attention	
Clarity of explanations and instructions	
Availability and organisation of apparatus for demonstration and class practical work	

Transitions from one activity to another

Awareness of what is going on

Response to pupils'
(a) work
(b) behaviour

Any pupils who particularly caught
your attention and why

Organising the clearing of apparatus after
practical work and settling the class

Ending a lesson
(a) Summary of lesson
(b) Packing up
(c) Exit from lab

C *Reviewing your observations*
Discuss your observations with the teacher with whom you have been during the day.

While all science teachers are required to teach the science syllabuses used in the school, each will have his or her own way of doing it. The relative use of different activities will probably vary between individual teachers, as will class management and interactions. List up to five points about this teacher's style which you feel you could incorporate into your own teaching style.

Make brief notes on your impressions of a science teacher's day. Try to make a list of the different types of job the teacher did during the day, and work out how much of the day was spent actually teaching.

For a detailed analysis of the secondary teacher's day, read the findings of the four-year survey edited by S. Hilsum and C. Strong: *The Secondary Teacher's Day*, NFER, 1978. This revealed that teachers worked on average 42½ hours per week. In addition, more than four hours were spent on school work at the weekend, and on average just over 1½ hours per holiday day. This gave a total of 40 hours per week over the whole year. Only a fifth of the working day was spent in face-to-face teaching. The rest was spent on associated tasks and administration: consultation 12%; mechanical tasks such as duplication, giving out paper and books, checking audio-visual apparatus, setting up other apparatus, 12%; supervision 11%; lesson planning 8%; marking and assessment, clerical tasks, administration, pupil welfare, emergencies, discipline, and reading associated with the job occupied the remainder.

The weekend work varied from nil to 28 hours, spent by about three-quarters of the teachers in planning lessons, marking, and doing general administrative and clerical tasks. Other weekend tasks included games matches, school functions and seeing parents.

**Topic 7
TEACHING MIXED
ABILITY SCIENCE
CLASSES**

Mixed ability groups are common, but mixed ability *teaching*, an advanced teaching skill, is difficult and rare. A number of recent reports have commented on the lack of differentiation in the work given to pupils of different ability during lessons with mixed ability classes. A common approach is to treat the class as a homogeneous whole and to teach at or just below the level of the average pupil in the class, ignoring the large differences between individuals. This is just as true in science as in other subjects. A typical science lesson with a first- or second-year class may start with a brief introduction, move on to pupils working in pairs, all using identical worksheets, and end with questions and a summary of the work done. The individual or group work in such a lesson typically involves the same task for all, so the same material is taught in the same way to all the pupils in the class. The teacher is aware of the extent of the ability range and the identity of children who are above or below average. In such a lesson, however, he or she is unable to do more than give brief extra attention to those who need a different approach, and this is more frequently to the slow learners than to the more able children.

What a teacher new to a school can do with mixed ability classes depends to a very great extent on what the department already does. Some teaching techniques which have been used successfully with mixed ability science classes are given below. You will notice that the techniques suggested are not mutually exclusive.

TECHNIQUES TO USE WITH MIXED ABILITY CLASSES

1 Whole-class teaching

Some examples of the appropriate use of whole-class teaching would be:
. . . Giving a lead-lesson with demonstrations and visual material to initiate a topic (could be done with several classes at once if the timetable allows)
. . . Giving a summary lesson
. . . Starting and ending a lesson or topic
. . . Emphasising safety
. . . Giving demonstrations
. . . Short spells designed to consolidate, inform, provide feedback
. . . Question and answer sessions, leading to discussion where all should be involved
. . . Showing a film, video or other visual material
. . . Organising a display or preparing for an outside activity.

2 Groupwork

Some examples of the use of small groups in a lesson are:
. . . planning and making a display
. . . discussion of problems set
. . . learning reading strategies (see Topic 5 in Part 1)
. . . practical work
. . . project work.

3 Circus of experiments

Here, one may select several ideas for practical work connected with a topic. The circus may last for one or more lessons. An example is a lesson on digestion with five stations of practical activities: a dismantled flannelgraph of human digestive system; a dismantled build-a-body model; a blackboard diagram with a labelling quiz; a simulated cow's stomach; starch/sugar investigation.

The class works in groups, each group progressing round the circus to include those experiments which suit the ability range within the group. (Such an experiment is described in detail in Kerry, T. and Sands, M.K., *Handling Classroom Groups*, Macmillan, 1982.)

4 Core and extension

In this case one could provide a basic core of material which everyone in the class has to follow, with extension work for the more able. Worksheets connected with the core can be produced for more than one level of ability, using different language levels, different diagrams and different types of question. Alternatively, common worksheets could have work at different levels. The extension work you provide should not be simply more of the same, but should involve the pupils in a different effort or activity.

Suitable work for the core, or a suitable approach to it should be provided for the less able. Pupils can work in small groups or individually.

The books in the series 'Biology for the Individual' (D. Reid and P. Booth, Heinemann, from 1970), are used successfully by teachers who wish to use a common core of material involving independent learning methods.

5 Topic-based approach

Each group works on a different aspect of the topic. Later the groups will come together to pool their learning.

6 Individualised learning

In this method pupils work alone with guidance from the teacher. The class follows the same topic, but individuals move through tasks selected for them, devised and put together to suit their own needs, abilities and attainment.

NB. The two related teaching methods of individual and individualised learning/teaching are often confused. Individual work is much more common and often consists of the same task, or essentially similar ones, for each member of the class, each child, however, working alone and at his or her own pace.

The subject of mixed ability teaching is a long and difficult one, and cannot be tackled fully in a workbook of this kind. For this reason we have added a full bibliography which you can work through as you have opportunity.

Meanwhile, Part 2 of this book takes you into the classroom to try out some practical teaching skills.

For Further Study

HMI series: Matters for discussion 6, *Mixed Ability Work in Comprehensive Schools*, HMSO, 1978
Kerry, T. and Sands, M.K., *Mixed Ability Teaching in the Early Years of the Secondary School*, Macmillan Education, 1982

Newbold, P., *The Banbury Report*, NFER, 1978

Reid, M., Clunies-Ross, L., Goacher, B., Vile, C., *Mixed Ability Teaching: Problems and Possibilities*, NFER-Nelson, 1981

Sands, M.K., 'Mixed ability science teaching: some current practices and problems', *School Science Review*, 1979, *60*, 213

Sands, M.K. and Kerry, T., *Mixed Ability Teaching*, Croom Helm, 1982

For bright and slow learners

Bell, P. and Kerry, T., *Teaching Slow Learners*, Macmillan Education, 1982

Kerry, T., *Teaching Bright Pupils in Mixed Ability Classes*, Macmillan Education, 1981

Kerry, T. (ed.), *Finding and Helping the Able Child*, Croom Helm, 1983

Mixed ability related to subject areas

Davies, R.P., *Mixed Ability Grouping*, Temple Smith, 1975

Kelly, A.V., *Case Studies in Mixed Ability Teaching*, Harper and Row, 1975

Wragg, E.C. (ed.), *Teaching Mixed Ability Groups*, David & Charles, 1976

Part 2

TEACHING SCIENCE

You will spend many hours teaching during your career. During this time you should continue to work at your teaching skills like a craftsman, quite deliberately seeking to improve them.

Part 2 of this workbook contains eight activities during which you will focus on some particular aspects of teaching science and on skills appropriate to a science teacher. Ultimately you are responsible for developing and evaluating your own professional competence. If you are still at the training stage you are able to call on the help of your tutor, teachers in the school and fellow students. More experienced teachers are encouraged to get together in pairs with colleagues, or to work with several other teachers in a department or Faculty.

The eight activities in this workbook are arranged, in fact, so that you *have* to approach fellow students, fellow teachers or tutors to help you. Do not feel threatened when these observers offer you advice. In teaching there is always a great deal to learn, even if you are fortunate enough to possess certain natural advantages. In any case it would be boring if you felt you had already reached a state of perfection, with no prospect of improving. Most teachers are aware that in the cut and thrust of classroom life there are frequent opportunities for rethinking one's approach.

The purpose behind this workbook is to provide some structure and a framework of advice within which you can develop personally throughout your career. There is deliberate overlap in the tasks observers are given. It is useful to have more than one view of some aspects of your teaching, and there is much merit in encouraging a more open approach within the profession.

Timetable

You need to organise yourself so that each of the eight tasks is completed. For students this is in itself a very important part of your training. Poorly organised teachers often come to grief. Do not wait for someone else to jog you into action, take the initiative yourself. Explain what is involved to the relevant observer and work your way through the set. Remember to follow up in each case as suggested.

More experienced teachers may feel that the opportunities for this kind of systematic observation are limited. But the eight Focuses can be used quite separately and in any order. As a qualified teacher with experience upon which to draw you will know which of these eight tasks require your more immediate attention, given your personal circumstances.

Focus	Title	Who observes
1	Lesson planning	A colleague
2	Reviewing resources in the science department	You
3	Teaching mixed ability classes in science	A colleague
4	Using group work in science lessons	A colleague
5	Encouraging experimental skills	A colleague
6	Developing pupils' thinking in science	You
7	Practising basic questioning skills	A colleague
8	Preparing, marking and analysing a test	You

Focus 1
LESSON PLANNING

What to do: Before the lesson and well before tackling this Focus, read section A. Check through section B. Then ask someone to observe you teaching the lesson and complete the Review Sheet in Section C. Discuss the comments made.

Section A   Some reminders about lesson preparation
Read this section well before you attempt this Focus.

Thinking things through. Research this topic (which will occupy a number of lessons, maybe some weeks) in detail, using a variety of books and other resources. Put what you have discovered into a logical teaching/learning sequence. A good set of notes on a topic will include syllabus outline, basic and enrichment information, diagrams, details of practicals and demonstrations, related visual material, problems to set pupils, examination questions and related examiners' comments, and homework suggestions. It can be filed intact for another occasion, when it can be adapted to suit another class.

Selecting and systematising. Divide the teaching/learning sequence into workloads for the class, each roughly a week long. Organise the material within each subsection to suit not only the total time at your disposal but also the length of each lesson and where it is placed in the day and in the week, the room you will be using, the number of minutes you will have just before the lesson and the number of children in the class.

Notes for each lesson. Having got to the outline lesson stage, now prepare each lesson for the week in detail. Your lesson plans or notes should help you feel more secure in front of a class. They should be long enough to guide you efficiently through the lesson but not so long that you become lost, or bogged down in a mass of detail. Some people prefer to keep their content notes on a topic intact and make references to the relevant sections in their lesson plan. Others prefer to intermingle lesson activities with the details of the information and skills being taught.

Different class constitutions, lesson arrangements, and so on, mean that the same content is rarely taught in the same way, or even the same order, twice.

With a separate set of well-prepared and documented notes on the topic you are teaching, your lesson plan can concentrate on the activities you and the class will be engaged in during the lesson. You can also check at a glance that you have a variety of activities and that none go on for too long. For a lesson plan of this nature, one or two sides of paper should be enough. In whatever way you prefer to write your plan, it should make these points clear:

Title: should state when and to whom the lesson is to be taught.

Aims: Try to state in a sentence or two the main things you are hoping the lesson will achieve. Give thought not only to the scientific content of your lesson but also to other objectives you wish to achieve. You may for example be concentrating on thinking skills (e.g. practice in data analysis and extrapolation) or on developing practical abilities (e.g. improving measuring skills).

Also note down any aims other than scientific ones, if relevant. You might, for example, be planning a lesson which will help you learn pupils' names, minimise control problems or encourage cooperation or initiative.

Activities through the lesson. Plan the lesson in clear stages. Make a note of the estimated time allowance for each stage. The procedures and activities from which you will select will include exposition, questioning, revision, demonstration, visual work on slides or film, individual or group work, practical work, reading, writing, drawing diagrams, tests and quizzes, games, computer work. Avoid more than ten minutes teacher-talk at any one time and keep as high a level of pupil activity and involvement as possible.

For many of these activities you will need to work out precisely how your material will be presented: what are the key questions, major points in your explanations, how children are to read the selected passages for best understanding, the title and format of the writing activities and how best to structure the drawing of diagrams.

Even if your lesson is planned for you in that, for example, you and the class are working from a worksheet prepared by the school, you should go through it and the associated practical work carefully in advance. In addition, you will also need to prepare your introduction to the lesson and worksheet, and the way in which you will summarise or draw the lesson together before the class leaves.

You must try out practical work before the lesson so that you can see that it works, estimate the time needed, modify your instructions, work out how group members might interact, and so on.

List of things needed and advance preparation. A separate list, clearly indicated in your notes for reference, is a help in a busy day. Such a list will probably also be in the technician's notebook and you can quickly check if you have everything you need. Things to be bought, grown or set up in advance of the lesson need a separate system.

Evaluation: to be completed after the lesson. It need not be lengthy. Try to strike a balance between class behaviour, teaching problems, and your own faults of planning or execution.

Section B   Checklist
When you have planned your lesson, go through and check the following points. Have you:
• decided how to get the class into the lab and settle them?
• got a good start to the lesson?
• shown in your lesson plan what the teacher and the pupils do and the amount of time planned for each activity?
• thought how to move from one activity to the next?
• made provision for bright and less able pupils in a mixed ability class?
• tried out the class practical work as well as your own demonstrations?
• decided how to give instructions?
• decided how to distribute and collect apparatus?
• produced for the lab technician a list of equipment needed?
• planned the summary or ending of the lesson?

Section C   Review Sheet
Now teach the lesson and have it observed, the observer filling in the review sheet which follows.

REVIEW SHEET

Summary of lesson-sequence and timing

Communication

Voice

Explaining

Giving instructions

Questioning

Worksheets and recording

Blackboard

Lesson-planning and structure

Aim

Control and management

Teaching procedures and pacing

Beginning and end of lesson

Use of resources

Transitions from one activity to another

Preparation

General

Content

Relationships

Amount of material

Knowledge and ideas

Practical work

Preparation

Organisation and management

Demonstrations

Follow-up

1 Discuss with the observer the comments made on the lesson.

2 Complete your evaluation of the lesson.

3 Before you forget how the lesson ended and what was achieved in it, make brief notes which will lead you into the planning of the next lesson.

**Focus 2
REVIEWING RESOURCES
IN THE SCIENCE
DEPARTMENT**

What to do: Consider the preparation, organisation, use and availability of resources in the department.

Discuss resources with the Head of Department then make notes using the headings given, adapting them where necessary to suit the particular circumstances of the department you are working in.

Books

What textbooks are used in class sets, either issued for occasional use or held by each child for the duration of the course?

Are they good? Are they up-to-date?

What reference books are used in preparing lessons, and for reference by pupils?

Do the pupils use the science books in the school library? If not, why not?

Worksheets

What school-produced worksheets or workcards and what commercially-produced sets are used in science teaching? What are they used for:
  (i) to give instructions for practical work,
  (ii) to give information,
  (iii) to set problems, questions or tests,
  (iv) to provide diagrams for copying and completion,
  (v) to cater specifically for above or below average children,
  (vi) to allow children to work at their own pace,
  (vii) to present additional exercises?

How are they used in any lessons you are currently observing?

Are you expected to use the worksheets in the same way as teachers with parallel classes?

Are you able to use worksheets other than the school's?

Are you able to add worksheets to the school collection, possibly helping to develop a part of the course?

Reprographics

Find out what reprographic machinery is available for teacher-use in the school.

Do you know how to use it properly for your own worksheets?

Is assistance available in typing masters and producing class sets of hand-outs? If so, find out how the system works.

Is there a limit to the amount of paper which may be used in duplicating?

Visual aids

List the visual aids machines, such as overhead projector, film loop, film and slide projectors, television, video-recorder, which are available and may easily be used in lessons. Find out what advance booking procedures apply.

What materials, such as acetate sheets and pens or film loops, are available for you to make your own visual aids?

Has the school ordered films during the term which you will be expected/able to use?

Describe how visual aids were used in any lessons you observed, and say why you think their use was effective.

Computer

What computers and programs are available for science classes?

How have they been used in any lessons you have observed?

Apparatus and equipment

As soon as possible, familiarise yourself with the equipment which is available in the science laboratories and prep rooms, as well as the procedure for requesting lab staff to prepare your practical requirements for lessons.

What catalogue or reference system is there for locating apparatus? Try to track down through the comprehensive list of equipment and the reference numbers to shelves or cupboards all the apparatus you need in a particular week.

How is apparatus for particular subject matter kept? For set experiments are all the necessary items kept together?

Where are the operating instructions for major pieces of apparatus?

What is the system for ordering apparatus for lessons?

What do you do if you find that you need something when you are teaching a lesson?

How do the technicians like apparatus left at the end of lessons? What action do you take if you find apparatus is unserviceable or consumable items are running low?

Remember that laboratory technicians are important members of the science team, and one of your first priorities should be to find out how the system works and what you should or can do to keep it working.

Other resources

Has the school a Resources Centre? If so, discover what facilities it offers.

Follow-up

1 Discuss with the other science teachers the points you have noted above, and their use of the resources available to them in the department.

2 Try to account for any differences between teachers in their use of resources. For example, do the differences relate to the age or ability of the classes taught, the topic being taught, the teacher's preferred teaching style, the experience of the teacher, the location of the lesson, the availability of technical help?

**Focus 3
TEACHING MIXED
ABILITY CLASSES IN
SCIENCE**

What to do: Select one of the topics you will shortly be teaching to a mixed ability class. Plan the lessons carefully so as to use and develop a number of the teaching methods suitable for use with a mixed ability class. Refer back to Topic 7 in Part 1 for suggestions; take into consideration in your planning the points you noted then and the insights you gained from your reading.

Ask an experienced teacher to observe one of these lessons and to comment on your ability to deal with mixed ability teaching using the headings overleaf.

1 Lesson preparation and organisation of materials before the lesson.

2 Use of: whole class teaching   core and extension
           group work   topic-based approach
           circus   individualised learning

3 Use of resources.

4 Effectiveness of worksheets or other material in allowing different approaches/activities by children of different abilities.

5 Suitability of work to the ability of the pupils.

6 Ability to identify slow and bright pupils.

7 Special provision for slow and bright pupils.

8 Evidence of effective record-keeping.

9 Strengths and weaknesses of the lesson.

Follow-up

1 Discuss with the observer the comments made on your lesson. How can you improve your skills for mixed ability teaching?

2 List the advantages and disadvantages you have experienced when using each of the teaching methods you selected.

3 Discuss with experienced teachers what they see as the problems associated with mixed ability teaching and the advantages to be gained from it. From your own experience note down your own feelings on the advantages and disadvantages of mixed ability grouping.

**Focus 4
USING GROUP WORK
IN SCIENCE LESSONS**

What to do: Plan a lesson (or a short series of lessons) which makes maximum use of group work. This could be a practical lesson where groups of two or more work together, either on identical practical work or different aspects of the same topic; project work; group discussion of a problem or of questions; group preparation of work and materials to be presented later; tackling a science game; preparing a dramatic incident to illustrate some aspect of science; or whatever other group activity seems suitable.

Before the lesson complete Section A. Ask someone to observe the lesson and complete Section B. After the lesson complete Section C.

Section A   Planning for group work

The most common use of group work in science lessons is in practical work, where pupils frequently work in pairs on the same task. This seems to be largely used as a variant of whole-class teaching, as little use is made of a differentiated approach, or of the different learning experiences which group work can give. Indeed, many science teachers would prefer individual practical work if the class were small enough and time and apparatus allowed it. Group work is not, in such a case, being used as a specific teaching strategy to achieve particular aims, but as a way of organising a class and the equipment available for a class activity.

Teachers' expectations are different, and reveal a gap between the ideal and the real situation. They see group work as encouraging cooperation and leadership among pupils, the exchange of ideas and views, pupils learning from and helping each other, and as an opportunity for pupils to work at their own pace on tasks suited to them. In fact this situation is not easy to achieve. However, with careful planning the teacher working with a group can stimulate higher levels of thinking and challenge pupils to predict, hypothesise, and draw conclusions.

Preparation before the lesson

1 Why are you using groups in this lesson?
Is it only because you have not enough equipment for each child to do the practical work alone? If so, start again.
Is it to encourage social skills such as cooperation, tolerance, learning from each other? Or is it to help you find out if different ability sub-groups accomplish different work as they work at different levels and pace? Or are you intending to spend some time stimulating different groups of pupils to different activities and different types of thinking? Is there some other reason?
Plan and structure your group work to try and achieve your aims.

2 How big will the groups be and how will they be formed? Your choice or the pupils'? Will they remain of the same composition for the whole period of group work (which could extend beyond one lesson)? Do you choose groups according to ability, interest, behaviour, friends?

3 Do you need to reorganise the furniture and teaching space to help?

4 Plan for a positive start to the lesson when you introduce the topic, set the scene, motivate the class and give instructions. Write down how you intend to start.

5 Ensure that each group has work at the right level, and that subject content and activities are geared to the groups' abilities.

6 What provision have you made for groups who finish early?

7 Plan a good end to the lesson, or series of lessons, which will draw the class together. What will it be: pooling and sharing of experience; commenting on things which went well or badly; reporting back from the groups; explaining noteworthy or spectacular outcomes; assessing what has been learned; looking forward to the next lesson; something else?

Section B
(To be completed by the observer during the lesson observed)

1 *Moving into group work* How are the groups composed? Is the transition into group work made smoothly?

2 *Tasks* What tasks are given to the group? Is the work geared to the ability of the group? Is the time spent on tasks high?

3 *Monitoring* Does the teacher monitor effectively and interact satisfactorily with each group? What are the teacher's major roles: e.g. teacher, motivator, helper, organiser?

4 *Trouble* How is potential trouble being avoided? Is the teacher vigilant, moving swiftly to groups where there are signs of unnecessary movement, too much chat, outbursts of noise? Are the quiet, hard-working groups ignored? Is the teacher easily visible? It is particularly important for safety reasons in practical science lessons that the teacher should be able to be identified instantly by a pupil looking round the lab. Is movement around the room easy? If an accident occurred would the teacher be able to move rapidly to it, or would the way be impeded (by stools, bags, knots of pupils)?

5 *Tracking* Track the teacher's movements from group to group for ten minutes, to see how long is spent with each group and how vigilant she or he is while talking to any one group.

6 *The internal organisation of the groups* Observe one or two groups closely during the lesson.
   (a) What are the pupils talking about? How does their talk affect the work being done? Are there one or more group members who assign work to the others and/or give instructions? Are there any disruptive members or those who do not wish to contribute to the task in hand? How much interactive talk, such as seeking or giving approval or help, is there? How much social off-task chat is there?

   (b) What kind of thinking seems to be going on in the group? Is the group involved at all in higher-level thinking such as interpretation, hypothesising, reasoning? Or is the talk simply to do with understanding and following instructions?

   (c) How much learning do you think is going on? Does the group work effectively together? Does it cohere?

Section C   Reviewing the lesson

1 Were you sufficiently prepared? Did you have to leave your monitoring of group work to deal with things which could or should have been done before the lesson?

2 Did you give the whole of your attention to the groups or did you allow individual children to come up with problems not connected with the work in hand? Did you disappear for a chat to the prep room, or sit at the desk and get on with some marking?

3 How much teaching and questioning did you do with each group? What other roles did you play: helper, motivator, consultant, discipline agent, organiser?

4 Were you quick enough in moving from group to group, or were groups waiting, unable to proceed, hands waving? If so, what did they do in this dead time? Were you harassed by demands? If so, is the class too dependent on you, or the work not of the sort which allows groups to proceed?

5 If boredom or chaos replaced a buzz of hard work, was it your fault because of inadequate preparation, poorly-designed tasks, lack of awareness of what the groups behind you were doing?

6 Were the groups who finished first involved in other activities as they waited? Were the slow-moving groups cajoled or helped into making faster progress?

Follow-up

1 Discuss your preparation and performance with the observer. Assess the success of the lesson and make suggestions for improvements or changes.

2 Try another group lesson, bearing in mind any points which were wrong in this one. Think again about aims and improve your preparation. Include activities which make the children think. Prepare carefully the material or activities for the ends of the ability range. Give particular thought to safety.

**Focus 5
ENCOURAGING
EXPERIMENTAL SKILLS**

What to do: Choose a lesson, or short series of lessons around a theme, in which the emphasis is on teacher demonstration and pupils' practical work. Read and act on Section A; this will help you think analytically about developing pupils' experimental skills. Complete column B in Section A. Now embark on your lesson(s).

During the course of your teaching ask a colleague to observe you at work and to complete the proforma in Section B. He or she should also complete Section C.

Section A   Developing Pupils' Experimental Skills
Experimental skills which you might be trying to develop in pupils during practical work are listed below, grouped loosely under four headings.

PR   Preparation for experiments
PF   Performance of experiments
EL   Elaboration of results
        (by processing the information obtained)
AC   Accounting for the results

Complete column B by listing one or more examples of each of the skills in column A. Build your checklist of skills into your lesson sequence.

COLUMN A		COLUMN B
	PREPARATION	
PR1	Put forward one or more hypotheses in connection with an experiment.	
PR2	Formulate the purpose of an experiment.	
PR3	Handle sources of information in connection with an experiment and extract the relevant information.	
PR4	Estimate sizes of quantities in an experiment.	

COLUMN A		COLUMN B
PR5	Devise methods or techniques of observation or measurement.	
PR6	Design apparatus for an experiment (may include drawing, depicting)	
PR7	Consider the ethical implications of experimentation.	
PR8	Carry out a pilot experiment.	
PR9	Sort out which quantities to vary, which to keep constant in an experiment.	
PR10	Decide on control or blank experiments.	
PR11	Consider the importance of safety in experimentation.	

PERFORMANCE

PF1	Choose the right apparatus or equipment for a given task.	
PF2	Use measuring instruments correctly.	
PF3	Follow instructions correctly.	
PF4	Record what occurs by means of notes, records, tables, drawings.	
PF5	Decide if there is a need to supplement or repeat results, giving reasons.	

ELABORATION

EL1	Carry out calculations on data, using appropriate aids where necessary.	
EL2	Represent data in different forms.	
EL3	Use and interpret graphs and charts.	

COLUMN A		COLUMN B
EL4	Look for trends, patterns, relationships in data.	
EL5	Classify data.	
	ACCOUNTING	
AC1	Interpret the relationships between results and hypotheses and predictions.	
AC2	Offer explanations for the results of experiments.	
AC3	Report on experiments orally or in writing.	
AC4	Offer suggestions for further experimentation.	

Section B Demonstrating

This section contains a list of skills a teacher should display when carrying out a demonstration experiment. Use this section as a checklist for your own preparation.

Then, ask your colleague to complete sections B and C when he or she observes you at work. In the Follow-up activities you will be able to check with your colleague how far you were successful in showing the skills listed here.

Demonstration: Observation Schedule

	very good	satisfactory	poor	very poor	COMMENT
PRACTICE (before the lesson)	4	3	2	1	
PUPIL POSITIONING (movement organised, all can see, seated, not too close to demo bench)	4	3	2	1	
TEACHER POSITIONING (Not obscuring, comfortable)	4	3	2	1	
VISIBILITY Size (big enough)	4	3	2	1	
Illumination (general light, light or dark background as appropriate)					
Height (raised if necessary, variation)	4	3	2	1	
SHOWING FIRST (*not* telling pupils what is going to happen before demo)	4	3	2	1	
DRAWING ATTENTION (to parts, events, so pupils see)	4	3	2	1	
PUPIL INVOLVEMENT (in helping with demo, question and answer)	4	3	2	1	
LOGICAL PRESENTATION	4	3	2	1	
SAFETY (pupil positions, screens, etc.)	4	3	2	1	

OTHER COMMENTS

Section C *(to the observer)*

The teacher will be trying to develop the skills shown in the checklists in Sections A and B above. Watch the teacher's interactions with individuals, groups and the whole class.

Use Sections A and B of this Focus to observe and comment on the teacher.

To what extent did the teacher include the skills listed in Section A?

Can you pick out any ways in which the development of these experimental skills in pupils could have been extended or improved?

How effective was the teacher as a demonstrator? What particular strengths and/or weaknesses were revealed by the checklist in Section B?

Follow-up

1 Discuss the lesson with the observer in the light of the observations made in sections B and C.

2 Following this discussion, write a brief critique of your work on experimental skills in this lesson and identify three aspects which you will try to improve.

3 Solomon, J., *Teaching Children in the Laboratory*, Croom Helm, 1980, is an interesting book to read on this topic.

**Focus 6
DEVELOPING PUPILS'
THINKING IN SCIENCE**

What to do: This Focus is designed to help you explore more effectively the thinking of your pupils about scientific concepts and issues. It asks you to use a clinical interview technique and explains how to prepare for and conduct the interview. Having read it, follow this sequence of events:

(a) Try out your interview on a colleague and amend anything which is unclear.
(b) Make an opportunity to interview several individual pupils.
(c) Carry out the interviews. Make notes about the pupils' responses as you proceed.
(d) Analyse the results and carry out Follow-up activities.

The work in this Focus involves you in talking to individual pupils about situations in science and is included:

- to help you to interact with individual pupils in class, particularly during practical work
- to give you insight into some aspects of pupils' thinking
- to enable you to get a better knowledge of the pupils' range of ability.

Choose one or more experiments related to work in one of the classes you teach, and prepare an individual interview to question children about them. Remember:

1 *Establish rapport* The pupils may be in an unfamiliar situation.

2 *State the purpose of the interview* Explain clearly but simply what you are going to do. You are not giving a test. The questions are about science and you would like him/her to attempt to answer them all.

3 *Clarify the starting point* To question pupils about the experiments in stages 4 and 5 you will have to make some assumptions about what the pupils know and understand. Check up on these assumptions – this enables you to begin with some easy questions.

4 *Introduce one or more experiments and probe the pupil's predictions* Before any manipulations are carried out, ask the pupil what he or she thinks will happen and why.

5 *Experiment(s) performed and pupil questioned* Either you, the pupil, or both can do the experiment. Asking what happened will probe observational skills; asking why will probe interpretation and understanding.

6 *Give feedback to the pupil* Give feedback to pupils immediately. They will react better to encouragement and praise than to criticism. Whether faults are corrected depends on the situation and what further experiments and questioning you wish to carry out.

7 *Repeat for other experiments, starting at 3 or 4.*

8 *Summarise* – summarise what you have done and give any further feedback. Then thank the pupil and end the interview.

The interview can conveniently be prepared to the following format:

STAGE	WHAT TO DO	SUMMARY OF WHAT TO SAY	RESULTS AND OBSERVATIONS
5	Pour liquid A on to liquid B	What can you see happening? Why do you think that has happened?	P noticed colour change but not precipitate. Said sometimes colours change when things get warm, but did not check until prompted to do so. No other ideas after this.

At each stage it may be necessary to use follow-up questions or *probes*. Try not to ask leading questions which tend to tell the pupil which answer you want (e.g. ones starting 'Don't you think that . . .').

Follow-up

1 What were the main misunderstandings which emerged in your interviews? Were any particularly surprising? How will this experience affect your teaching of these topics?

2 Look at some of the questions and responses in the reports produced by the Assessment of Performance Unit for the Department of Education and Science (DES) and published by HMSO. The small cheap paperbacks in the Science Reports for Teachers series are particularly useful. They are available from the Association for Science Education.

3 Some interesting 'Science Reasoning Tasks' were developed by the Concepts in Secondary Mathematics and Science Project (CSMS). They are available from the National Foundation for Educational Research.

4 The work of the CSMS project on science is reported in Shayer, M. and Adey, P., *Towards a Science of Science Teaching*, Heinemann Educational Books, 1981.

5 Driver, R., *The Pupil as Scientist*, Open University Press, 1983.

6 A very interesting series of booklets is being produced by the Children's Learning in Science project. These are available from the Centre for Science Education, University of Leeds. They explore pupils' understanding of particular topics.

Focus 7
PRACTISING BASIC
QUESTIONING SKILLS

What to do: Read the checklist in Section A, and practise the questioning skills in the checklist through several lessons. Ask an observer to watch a lesson and comment on your questioning skills using the proforma provided in Section B.

Section A   Questioning skills
Read the points given below and practise them in a number of lessons. About one-third of all teacher-talk to classes consists of questions. Why do teachers ask questions? To motivate, to revise, to find out what pupils know or remember, to monitor the teaching, to gain feedback on learning, to make pupils think, to encourage them to use words, to encourage problem solving, to help pupils learn from each other — these are a few of the reasons.

Checklist
1 *Key questions* These are the main questions which will take you through a sequence, lead the class to explore a new topic, or take pupils from facts to thinking. They need to be worked out in advance, as they are difficult to frame on the spur of the moment.

2 *Distribution of questions* Teachers usually face the whole class whether in a lab or a classroom. The keen pupils (squares in the diagram) tend to sit immediately in front of the usual teaching position; the less keen, possibly lower ability, pupils (circles) tend to gravitate to the back corners; those who prefer to be quiet and relatively untroubled by the teacher (triangles) choose the sides and mid-back. The teacher's arc of vision takes in the squares, and it needs a conscious effort to turn to the right or left-hand corners. Consider the implications of this, *and consciously try to distribute your questions*. Questions and answers tend to be rapid and accurate with pupils *inside* the teacher's scan. Slow or inaccurate responses from elsewhere act as little reinforcement for a teacher anxious to get on with the lesson.

Move round the room and talk from different positions to give you access to different groups and increase your awareness of the possible contributions of all the pupils in the class.

3 *Eye contact* Look a pupil in the eyes when you ask a question and listen to the answer. But keep your antennae moving round everyone else.

4 *Timing, prompting and reinforcement* In trying to involve particular pupils, ask a question, pause to give everyone time to think, then add the pupil's name. New teachers tend to allow too little time in the pause for pupils to think.

When someone gets it wrong, or doesn't answer, pass the question to someone else, but try to remember to come back to the first pupil later with a different question.

Use pupil responses positively. Praise or make a welcoming comment where possible. Don't belittle, or be sarcastic, threaten or punish, or laugh at a pupil.

5 *Vocabulary and clarity* The language you use should be at the right level and unambiguous to the pupils.

6 *Non-verbal cues* Pupils will watch for, and act on, non-verbal cues from you indicating encouragement, enthusiasm, understanding, puzzlement and other emotions.

Patterning of questions

Section B   Teaching a lesson using questioning skills
To the observer
Use the list below to comment on the teacher's use of questioning skills during the lesson observed. Write down questions which showed good and bad practice, using these headings:

1 *Key questions*
Use the list of key questions worked out before the lesson to check the use of this sequence of questions as the lesson proceeds.

2 *Distribution of questions*
Make a plan of the class. For a specified period of time in the lesson tick each pupil's name or position as the class is questioned. After the lesson discuss the distribution of questions and consider how effectively the whole class was involved.

3 *Eye contact*
Does the teacher make effective eye contact, while still being aware of the rest of the class?

4 *Timing*
Does the teacher wait long enough for an answer? Does he or she seize too quickly on what the pupil says without giving time for a considered response? Are several questions asked without pause for a reply?

5 *Prompting*
Are pupils who say they don't know encouraged to try again (possibly later)? Does the teacher rephrase or simplify the question or go back a few steps, or give clues? Does he or she ask for a second opinion, even when the first is correct? Does he or she genuinely appear to want to know the answer?

6 *Reinforcement*
Does the teacher praise or reward good answers, and build up on half answers? Does he or she try to avoid rejecting an answer completely?

7 *Vocabulary and clarity*
Is the language at the right level? Are the questions clearly phrased?

8 *Non-verbal clues*
Is the teacher able to use non-verbal behaviour to back up his or her use of questions?

Follow-up

1 Discuss with the observer your questioning skills and how you can improve them.

2 Tape-record a later lesson and consider how far you have developed the skills mentioned above.

3 Observe an experienced science teacher teaching a problem-solving lesson. Note down all the questions used which are designed to make the pupils think.

4 Read the chapter by G.A. Brown in Wragg, E.C. (ed.), *Classroom Teaching Skills*, Croom Helm, 1984; and Kerry, T., *Effective Questioning*, Macmillan Education, 1982.

**Focus 8
PREPARING, MARKING
AND ANALYSING A TEST**

What to do: Prepare and mark a test for a class of more than 24 pupils using the technique described in section A. Carry out an analysis of this test as described in section B.

Section A Preparing and marking a test
A test should be structured to reflect the knowledge content, skills and processes which have been taught.

1 Divide the knowledge content into a number of areas (a maximum of six).

2 Decide on a simple categorisation system for the objectives of the test with, say, four categories, for example:
   recall – remembering knowledge learned;
   comprehension and understanding – processing information learned before an answer can be given;
   using *skills, techniques, processes* in familiar situations;
   application of knowledge, skills, processes, techniques in unfamiliar situations.

3 Draw up a grid with these two sets of categories on the two axes:

	Areas of knowledge content					
	A	B	C	D	E	F
recall							x
comprehension							x
skills, techniques, processes							x
application							x

x x x x x x

55

4 Enter at x the number of marks for each category.

5 Choose or write the questions. Give marks to each part of a question and write them in the appropriate box on the grid, making quick decisions. Try to get the overall mark distribution reasonably close to your original estimates.

6 Draw up a mark scheme. Try to allocate marks for specific points. In open-ended questions or those testing application, leave some flexibility to reward good answers which may not quite fit your scheme.

7 When the test has been completed by the pupils, try out your mark scheme on a few answers. Amend if necessary. Then mark the tests. Note the advice on marking and feedback given on pages 22-5.

Section B Analysing a test

Analysis of a test can
- help the teacher to improve his or her teaching skills
- help to diagnose pupil difficulties
- help to improve the test for re-use on another occasion
- enable the test to be refined and made more suitable for its purposes. For example, if the results are to be used to help with important decisions involving the differences between pupils (e.g. banding and setting, examination entries, careers advice), the test should distinguish reliably and fairly between pupils.

The procedure below will allow you to analyse the test for these purposes:

1 Find the mean (average) mark per pupil and the standard deviation of the marks.

2 If sizeable numbers of pupils are involved, show the mark distribution visually on a simple histogram.

3 Divide the completed tests into two piles, the 50% of pupils with the highest total marks and the 50% with the lowest marks (discarding the central one if there is an odd number of pupils).

4 Find the total marks obtained for each question by the pupils in the top and bottom 50%. To illustrate the calculation, if there were twelve pupils for question 1:

Marks / 10 (top) $9+4+7+3+6+1 = 30$
Marks / 10 (bottom) $4+7+2+6+5+3 = 27$

The *facility* of the question is found by dividing the total marks obtained by all pupils (30 + 27) by the maximum possible marks (12 × 10),

i.e. here the facility = $\dfrac{30 + 27}{12 \times 10} = 0.48$

A very simple measure of the *discrimination* of the question is given by the difference between the marks obtained by the top and bottom 50%, i.e. here $30 - 27 = +3$.

5 Consider the test as a whole. For greatest effectiveness at distinguishing between pupils, a test should have a mean mark of about 50% of full marks and a standard deviation of about 1/6 of full marks. You would expect the marks to be fairly well-spread, with more pupils in the central band than at the extremes. How do the results of your test compare with these ideals? Are there any diagnostic messages to be obtained from the results (e.g. a group of pupils who are very weak on the topic)?

6 Look critically at individual questions.

(a) Are there any questions with very high or very low facilities? These will not contribute much to distinguishing between pupils, but are they useful for other reasons? What do the very low facilities suggest (e.g. question too difficult, a topic not taught well)?

(b) Are there any questions with negative, zero or low positive discriminations? In general you might expect sizeable positive discriminations, since pupils who do well in the whole test are likely to do well in individual questions.

Can you suggest reasons for the exceptions (e.g. bad wording of question)? Make a note of questions which seem unsatisfactory for this or other reasons.

(c) Are there any common errors or misconceptions which have been revealed by the test? How do you think these might have arisen?

Follow-up

If interesting errors or misconceptions are revealed, it might be possible to arrange some individual interviews along the lines indicated in Focus 6, to probe the reasons for them.

Part 3   REFLECTIONS ON EXPERIENCE

The third section of this workbook contains five topics which examine, in the light of practical experience in school, some areas already discussed in Part 1, as well as adding some new lines of thought to help bridge the gap between theory and practice.

Topic A asks you to take stock of your teaching, your use of resources, and to review your teaching style, and thus relates to a number of areas touched on earlier. Topic B on scientific vocabulary adds to the work done earlier on reading, and writing worksheets. Topic D asks you to consider your marking and assessment, and thus builds on the work in both Part 1 and Part 2.

Current issues in science education, issues which are of fundamental importance in the current debate on the school curriculum and developments in science teaching are considered in Topic C, while the organisation and management of a science department are discussed in Topic E, raising points which will become important to you as your responsibility and role in decision-taking within the school increase.

The work in Part 3 can be done alone, as a member of a group in school, or as part of an initial or in-service course.

Topic A
TAKING STOCK

At the end of a term, look back over your lessons and your other activities in school and evaluate your strengths and weaknesses. Your conclusions may affect the planning you do for the next term's work and even the type of school you would wish to move to next. This Topic looks first at your own view of yourself as a teacher, then at your use of resources in your teaching. Thirdly, it asks you to consider your style of teaching, and finally to arrange a discussion with your Head of Department to discuss your performance and potential.

Activity 14:
How do you rate yourself as a teacher?

Evaluate yourself for each item in Table 6 below to give a profile showing your strengths and weaknesses.

TABLE 6: A SELF-ANALYSIS PROFORMA

	Good			Poor
	4	3	2	1
Preparation:				
Lesson planning				
Advance preparation				
Knowledge of subject-matter				
Management:				
Class control				
Gaining attention				
Keeping attention				
Communication:				
Skill in explaining				
Ability to give instructions				
Questioning skills				
Rapport with classes				
Relationships with pupils				
Teaching techniques:				
Use of individualised work				
Use of group work				
Use of blackboard				
Using visual aids				
Ability to write worksheets				
Skill with demonstrations				
Use of practical work				
Knowledge of laboratory safety				
Evaluation:				
Evaluation and analysis of lessons				
Response to advice				
Assessment:				
Recognition of pupils' difficulties				
Marking				
Record-keeping				
Attitudes and relationships:				
Contribution to the department				
Relationships with other science staff				
Contribution to life of school				
Enthusiasm				
Initiative				
Commitment to teaching				

Activity 15:
Using resources

Do you know how to use the equipment available to you in the school? Have you used it effectively in your teaching? Use the proforma in Table 7 to assess your performance over the last term.

TABLE 7: EFFECTIVENESS OF RESOURCE USE

	Good 4	3	2	Poor 1
Blackboard				
Overhead projector				
16 mm film projector				
Film loop projector				
Film strip projector				
Slide projector				
TV				
Videotape recorder				
Tape recorder				
Computer				
(a) knowledge and use of available programs				
(b) programming				
Typewriter				
Reprographic equipment: photocopier				
spirit duplicator				

Finally, have you been making, collecting and classifying material of use to you: pictures, magazine articles, reprints, photographs, worksheets, catalogues, addresses, charts, OHTs, slides, computer programs? YES   NO
Can you find what you want when you want it? YES   NO

Activity 16:
Reviewing your teaching style

Use the questions that follow to review your own teaching style:

1 Firstly, consider the reasons for liking or disliking particular classes.

Which class did you enjoy teaching most and least?

Which of the following factors influenced your answer?
Age of pupils   Scientific content
Average ability level of pupils   Individual pupil behaviour
Range of ability of pupils   General class attitude
Timing of lessons   Others:
Rooms you taught in

2 Research evidence shows that a teacher develops a style of teaching and tends to use this style regardless of the age and ability of the class being taught. What is *your* style so far? Is it one you approve of? If not, what other teaching activities do you need to start actively incorporating in your lessons? To answer these questions work through the next few paragraphs systematically.

(a) From your lesson notes for a reasonable block of time (say two weeks), briefly summarise each lesson you taught in terms of teaching and learning activities, such as class practical, teacher demonstration, discussion, groupwork, project work, teacher talk, questioning, class writing, reading. As you do so, note the approximate amount of time you spent per lesson on each activity.

(b) In year groups or in subject divisions, list all the teaching activities you used during the two-week period, and the total number of hours you spent on each.

(c) How much does your teaching style vary between year groups and between subjects if you teach more than one?

(d) What is your overall profile of teaching activities?

(e) Now go through the notes on your list once more; or for any one class go through the activities you have asked them to do during the term. Divide the tasks into *low-level tasks* (such as drawing, copying, taking dictated notes, reading, looking up information, learning facts, doing practical work following instructions, answering straightforward questions, writing up practical work, filling in missing words, simple comprehension), and *high-level tasks* (such as collecting evidence, solving problems, data analysis, hypothesising, drawing own conclusions, evaluating).

Are you satisfied with the results of your analysis? If not, what are you going to do about it?

3 Find the lesson notes for the best-managed and the most disastrous lessons you taught in the last three weeks:

Why was the best lesson such a success?	Why was the worst lesson such a failure?
Careful planning	Poor planning
Interesting subject matter	Depressed teacher performance
Your own enthusiasm	Unsupportive class attitudes
Good pupil attitudes	Poor class or individual behaviour
Good pupil behaviour	Unfortunate incident
Other (name)	Other (name)

Return to Topic 2 in Part 1 on class management and control and review your methods of control. Write an honest evaluation of your management and control methods, making use of your review of Topic 2. Formulate a policy for next term, and include a summary of it in your account. Insert your account in this book.

**Activity 17:
Obtaining a second
opinion about your teaching**

Finally, having taken stock of yourself, ask your head of department or some other senior teacher to review with you your performance and to discuss your potential.

You may be in a school where there is a staff appraisal system. The term may sound threatening, but it is not concerned with pointing out where you have gone wrong, but is essentially a positive thing designed to look at your *performance* on the job and how it might be improved, and your *potential*, both in the school and in your career.

Even if your school has no such system, you could discuss the same points with your immediate boss. Fix a meeting in advance, in a place where you will be undisturbed and unrushed. Agree beforehand on a list of points (see below) you would like to cover and ask the other person to collect or refer to any relevant documents (some schools now use job descriptions) and to plan the interview in broad terms, so as to enable an open discussion and *exchange* of ideas to take place.

A number of points from the previous Activities may have occurred to you as worthy of discussion. Here are a few more for consideration:

- Those parts of the job where you feel most/least effective and competent, and whether best use is made of your particular talents and interests.
- Your degree of job satisfaction.
- Your total contribution to the department's work.
- The amount of responsibility and autonomy given to you, your involvement in decision-making in the department, and your possible contribution to future developments.
- Your relationships with pupils and other science teachers.
- Within the school, your contributions and attitudes to pastoral care, extracurricular activities, teaching in other subject areas, remedial classes, examination classes.
- Your hopes for future career development, both in the near future and more long-term.
- Any need for professional development in and outside the school, including further training and wider experience.

At the end of the interview, both people should agree on any action which is needed, and take steps to see that it happens. Examples are: some sixth-form teaching next year, absence for a relevant in-service course, more work in the house system.

Write below the action decided:

For Further Study

Bowley, R.L., *Teaching without tears*, Centaur Press, 1961

Eggleston, J.F., Galton, M. and Jones, M., *A Science Teaching Observation Schedule*, Schools Council Research Studies, Macmillan Education, 1975

Eggleston, J.F., Galton, M. and Jones, M., *Processes and Products of Science Teaching*, Schools Council Research Studies, Macmillan Education, 1976

Francis, P., *Beyond control*, George Allen and Unwin, 1975

Galton, M. and Eggleston, J.F., 'Some characteristics of effective Science teaching', *European Journal of Science Education*, 1979, 1, No. 1, pp. 75-86

Saunders, M., *Class control and behaviour problems*, McGraw-Hill, 1979

Wragg, E.C., *Classroom teaching skills*, Croom Helm, 1984

Topic B
SCIENTIFIC
VOCABULARY

Science teachers need to take particular care with the vocabulary they use in science lessons because of the difficulties that scientific subject matter poses.

Specialist scientific words
Words which denote real objects or entities (e.g. meniscus, thorax) can be illustrated by the objects themselves, pictures, drawings or models. Sometimes there is an everyday synonym which is helpful, at least in the early stages of learning a new word. Processes (e.g. evaporation, photosynthesis) are more tricky. Obviously it helps if you can show the process taking place and/or use models or flow diagrams. But the relationship between the meaning of the word and what the pupils actually see is often a complex one. Pupils need help to abstract the idea from the experience. Words which denote scientific concepts (e.g. energy, wavelength, element, compound) and mathematical concepts frequently used in science (e.g. rate, ratio, proportionality) require more extended treatment. Pupils need a number of experiences of a concept in a variety of circumstances. Also the relationship of the concept to the experience needs to be explained and discussed, with time being allowed for the pupils to work with and assimilate the ideas involved. If the word for the concept is used in everyday language with a different or less specific meaning (e.g. fruit, energy) then particular care must be taken to explain the similarities and differences between the two uses of the word.

Non-technical words
There are many other words used in the teaching of science which cause difficulties for pupils even though teachers would not consider them to be specialist scientific words. Some work for the Australian Science Education Project (Gardner, 1972) is useful in this connection. The list which follows is taken from it. It shows the percentage of first-year Australian secondary pupils (age about 12) who correctly answered a multiple choice question on the meaning of the word, giving a crude measure of its difficulty for pupils at this level. The length of the list shows the problems an unwary teacher may cause by injudicious use of what to him or her is normal vocabulary.

Activity 18:
Thinking about vocabulary

Read the list below and note which apparently common words can cause difficulty. Think of synonyms and explanatory phrases that could be used to aid communication and improve vocabulary.

TABLE 8: LIST OF NON-TECHNICAL WORDS

(10-19% correct)	disintegrate	
	random	
	spontaneous	
(20-29% correct)	rate	
	symmetrical	
(30-39% correct)	average	
	concept	initial
	conception (of baby)	latitude (geographical)
	contract (get smaller)	law
	converse (opposite)	lubricate
	correspond (matching)	negative
	descendant	partial
	factor	revise
	grain (of rocks)	valid

(40-49% correct)	action	incident (light)
	algebra	incline
	audible	invert
	component	omit
	composition	percentage
	constituent	perpendicular
	consume	positive (number)
	crude	relative (in size)
	diameter	sense
	diversity	standard
	effect	stimulate
	efficient	tabulate
	emit	topic
	illuminate	
(50-59% correct)	arid	negligible
	complex	neutral
	continent	outline
	contrast	phenomenon
	contribute	plot (graph)
	converge	probability
	crest	recoil
	devise	regulate
	dominant	repel
	external	represent
	fundamental	residue
	illustrate	resist
	immerse	row (table)
	interpret	sequence
	liberate	simultaneous
	linear	symbol
	magnitude	textbook
	minimum	vessel
	modify	
(60-69% correct)	accumulate	molten
	adjust	naked
	alternate	obvious
	analysis	oppose
	aperture	origin
	calculate	positive (result)
	coincide	previous
	column	primary
	conical	primitive
	consecutive	process
	consistent	profile
	convention	propagate
	criticise	proportion
	deflect	pump
	degree (unit)	reference
	descend	reflect
	detect	regular
	device	relevant
	diagonal	resource
	disperse	retard
	displace	rigid
	enable	section (biology)
	essential	sensitive (to light)
	excite	stagnant
	exclude	stain
	exert	substitute

film (layer)
fog
generate
impact
influence
involuntary
irritate
isolate
limit
logic
maximum

suckle
suspend
technical
tend
theory
thrust
treatment
vertical
violet
vital

(70-79% correct)

ability
absence
abundant
accurate
adjacent
agent
agriculture
annual
appropriate
associate
assume
automatic
bounce
boundary
brittle
capable
characteristic
coarse
conclusion
constant
convert
cultivate
decay
define
derive
dimension
distinct
distribute
edible
elastic (stretching)
erect
estimate
evacuate
exact (precise)
exception
excess
expel
expose
extreme
grind
imagination
index
inflate
instantaneous

intake
internal
junction
layer
level (surface)
manufacture
mature
mild
multiple
neglect
observation
penetrate
permanent
predict
preparation
presence
proof
refine
relationship
respond
rub
rule (regulating behaviour)
scale (of instrument)
sensitive (instrument)
sign (+, −)
simplify
smear
source
spiral
submerge
successive
system
table (of numbers)
tension
tide
transform
tropic
tube
typical
uniform
unique
vocal
wedge
wilt

Activity 19:
Paying attention to
scientific vocabulary

Cloze procedure lets you check a textbook with the pupils who use it: you can predict their ability to use the text and also see if they understand both the language and the scientific content. The pupils have to read carefully to get the sense of the passage. The procedure is thus concerned not just with vocabulary but language more generally. It provides a useful starting point for increasing your awareness of pupils' difficulties.

1 Select a passage of about 200 words from the textbook to be used with a class. Delete either every seventh word or all the nouns (or verbs). Type the passage, leaving spaces for the deletions. Ask pupils to fill in the spaces. Get pupils to check the completed passage and find the number of correct completions (or acceptable alternatives). Over 65% correct means that the pupil can understand the text and use it to work from. 40-65% means help will be needed. Below 40% means that the textbook is too difficult to use.

2 Give the results of the cloze exercise.

3 In preparing a lesson for a first or second-year class:

(a) List the specialist scientific words you will use. Decide what techniques are needed to help pupils with them.

(b) Scan the list given above of non-specialist words. Mark those which you might use in the lesson. If the words are likely to prove difficult decide how to help the pupils to understand them, or how to avoid their use.

(c) If possible, give an observer copies of your lists and ask him/her to concentrate on your use of language in the lesson, paying particular attention to the words you have identified.

Topic C
THE SCIENCE
CURRICULUM

In recent years there has been considerable debate about the nature of the science curriculum. Many documents have contributed to this, some of them produced by the Department of Education and Science (DES), the Association for Science Education (ASE) and the Royal Society. The national importance of the science curriculum is further illustrated by the fact that a project fundamentally concerned with the issue, the Secondary Science Curriculum Review (SSCR), is one of the few large projects to have survived the changes in the Schools Council.

It is often not easy to translate the general statements in such documents into policies and strategies for a particular science department. Activity 20 aims to help with this process.

The underrepresentation of girls in the physical sciences is a cause of considerable concern to many people involved in science education. They argue that the nation is thereby deprived of a significant contribution to its scientific, engineering and technological activity and that many girls cut themselves off from physical-science related careers at a very early stage. Activity 21 asks you to consider this issue.

Activity 20:
Where should the
curriculum be going?

1 Read carefully through the complete instructions for this Activity.
2 Obtain as many recent documents on the science curriculum as you can and read the parts particularly concerned with the 11-16 age range. (Some suitable extracts are given at the end of the Topic.)
3 Examine the list of contrasting statements given in Table 9 below. They represent some dimensions along which it might be said that the science curriculum has varied in the past.
4 In the light of your reading, identify any additional pairs of statements which are needed to represent the changes proposed.
5 Think about the school in which you have done your most recent teaching. On the horizontal lines between contrasting statements indicate with a vertical line where you feel this school stands on the issue. Leave blanks if you feel unable to judge.
6 Add an arrow to your vertical lines to show the direction in which you feel the school ought to be changing, making the length of the arrow indicate how much you think the change is needed. Add notes if you wish.
7 What do you feel are the most urgent and important changes for the science department to attend to?

TABLE 9: THE SCIENCE CURRICULUM

ABOUT SCIENCE

	10	0	10	
Emphasis on science as a body of knowledge, with little attention to the processes of science	10	0	10	Emphasis on science as a way of knowing and on the processes of science
Science is a unity	10	0	10	The separate sciences are very different from each other
Pure science for its own sake	10	0	10	Applied science for its utility
An analytical approach to science	10	0	10	A descriptive approach to science

CURRICULUM CONTENT

	10	0	10	
Emphasis on the basic facts				Emphasis on models and theories
Wide coverage, giving an idea of the extent of scientific knowledge	10	0	10	Narrower coverage, a few topics being taught in depth to a level where pupils understand
Needs of the pupil as a basis for choosing content	10	0	10	Needs of the nation or the nature of science itself as a basis for choosing content

AIMS

	10	0	10	
Science education develops pupils as people to take their place in society	10	0	10	Science education develops people who are intellectually competent in science
Science is for the more able	10	0	10	Science is for all
Science education should show the world as it is	10	0	10	Science education looks to the future

CURRICULUM DEVELOPMENT

	10	0	10	
National responsibility for curriculum development	10	0	10	Local or school responsibility for curriculum development
Curriculum development gradual, by refinement and revision	10	0	10	Curriculum development by reform and innovation

TEACHING METHODS

	10	0	10	
Whole class learning	10	0	10	Group or individual learning
Teaching facts	10	0	10	Teaching concepts
Practical work to show, to verify	10	0	10	Practical work to discover, to raise problems, to develop skills
Learning by pupils depends mostly on their ability	10	0	10	Learning by pupils depends on the way we teach them
Learning is passive, receptive	10	0	10	Learning is active, involved
Pupils have to be given information properly if they are to learn	10	0	10	Pupils have to interact with materials in order to learn
Sequence of learning materials reflects the logical structure of the material	10	0	10	Sequence of learning materials reflects the way pupils think and learn

Assessment, emphasising recall, facts		Assessment emphasising understanding, concepts, applications
	10 0 10	

Assessment emphasising knowledge		Assessment emphasising skills
	10 0 10	

Activity 21:
Girls and Science

1 Study the tables given below. (The figures refer to 1978-79 and 1980.) What strikes you about the figures? Do you think it is reasonable to view the underrepresentation of females in many parts of these tables as a problem?

2 Obtain as many recent documents on the issue of girls and science as you can. Some suggestions are given at the end of the topic.

3 Read the material and list ideas for action in your school which might persuade more girls to take up science.

TABLE 10: THE NUMBER OF FEMALES FOR EVERY MALE STUDYING SCIENCE SUBJECTS AT VARIOUS LEVELS IN THE EDUCATION SYSTEM IN ENGLAND AND WALES, 1978-79

	Attempt CSE	Attempt O-level	Attempt A-level	Obtain first degree	Do post-graduate research	Obtain PhD
Biology	2.22	1.69	1.19	0.78	0.40	0.30
Mathematics	1.05	0.80	0.33	0.39	0.13	0.13
Chemistry	0.61	0.59	0.45	0.26	0.19	0.13
Physics	0.19	0.32	0.23	0.13	0.11	0.09
All subjects	1.01	1.03	0.87	0.56	0.29	0.19

Taken from the Royal Society/Institute of Physics report *Girls and Physics* Table 1 (see reference list).

TABLE 11: PUPIL SUBJECT CHOICES IN YEARS 4 AND 5 (1980)

	Percentages			
Subject choices	Boys		Girls	
Bio., Chem. and Phys.	14		9	
3 subjects Total		14		9
Bio. and Chem.	3		10	
Bio. and Phys.	7		4	
Chem. and Phys.	14		3	
2 subjects Total		24		17
Bio. only	7		33	
Chem. only	2		3	
Phys. only	18		3	
One subject Total		27		39
General Science	13		10	
Human Biology	2		11	
Other combinations	12		0	
Total		27		21
No science	7		14	

APU, *Science in Schools, Age 15, Report no. 1* (1982), quoted in *Science Education 11-16: Proposals for Action and Consultation* (see reference list)

References and Further Study

ASE, 'Education through science: The policy statement of the Association for Science Education, 1981', *School Science Review*, 1981, **63**, 222, particularly pages 10, 16-19

DES, *Science Education in Schools: A Consultative Paper*, 1982, particularly paras 16-22

Harding, J., *Switched Off: the Science Education of Girls*, Longman, 1983

Hearn, M., 'Girls for Physical Science: A school-based strategy for encouraging girls to opt for the physical sciences', *Education in Science*, April 1979

Joint Physics Education Committee of the Royal Society and the Institute of Physics, *Girls and Physics*, Institute of Physics, 1982

Lillis, K.M. and West, R.W., *Issues in Science Education: A bibliographic survey*, Association for Science Education, 1984

Royal Society, *Science Education 11-18 in England and Wales, A Report in Summary*, 1982 Royal Society, particularly paras 20-29

Secondary Science Curriculum Review, *Science Education 11-16: proposals for action and consultation*, 1983

Smail, B., Whyte, J., Kelly, A., 'Girls into Science and Technology: the first two years', *School Science Review*, 1982, **63**, 225

The Secondary Science Curriculum Review will be publishing a variety of useful documents over the next few years. Useful initial references are:

'Outline of the purpose, organisation and operation of the Review', *Secondary Science Curriculum Review*, 1983

SSCR Newsletter No. 1, Summer 1984

**Topic D
REFLECTIONS ON
ASSESSMENT**

The activities in this Topic are designed to help you to reflect on some important aspects of assessment.

Activity 22 concentrates on your own approach to day-to-day assessment activities in school. Are you carrying these out as effectively as possible?

Activities 23 and 24 focus on the issue of *what* is being assessed. The first of these draws your attention to the very interesting work which the Assessment of Performance Unit is doing. The second suggests a technique by which you can get a better understanding of what examination boards mean by the statements of objectives in their syllabuses.

**Activity 22:
Setting, marking and
record-keeping**

Carry out an appraisal of the effectiveness of your approach to setting and marking work and to keeping records on pupils. Use the following questions to help you. Remember that definite but limited targets for self-improvement are more likely to be successful than generalised pious hopes.

1 Do you set homework regularly?

2 Do you mark and return written homework quickly? If not can you identify (say) three things you could do to improve?

3 Do you set tests often enough to monitor pupils' progress and provide motivation?

4 What is your opinion of the quality of your own tests? Can you state (say) three ways in which you could improve them?

5 When marking or correcting work do you
(a) generally try to encourage and help . . .
(b) . . . but take a stronger line if necessary?
(c) make constructive comments on the work?
(d) correct errors – but not so many as to discourage pupils completely?
(See also Topic 4 in Part 1.)

6 Do pupils generally react well when you give back marked work? If not, why not?

7 Have you been caught out recently on your knowledge of an individual pupil? Why did this happen? What steps might you take to make sure the experience is not repeated?

8 Do you have a system for recording some or all of the following about each pupil?
attainment, effort, motivation, practical skills, understanding, behaviour.

9 Some schools use record sheets which have categories of this kind together with a simple scale. Would a record sheet like this be helpful to you? How could it be made detailed enough to be useful, but simple enough for you to have the time to use it?

10 Increasingly, schools are devising and using profiles to record behaviour, progress and achievement of pupils. There are many different profiles reflecting different views of which attitudes, skills and abilities the school should be recording. Some of these ask pupils to carry out their own self-assessment.

It is important that profiles are constructed so that those completing them can respond to well-defined statements. The table shown for recording pupil attitudes is an example of this. Implied questions like 'Does the pupil usually cooperate with staff?', while subjective, do nevertheless ask something specific. Any profile, however, must be a compromise between accuracy and completeness on the one hand and practicality on the other.

Try out this attitude profile on one of your classes.

TABLE 12: EXAMPLE OF A PROFILE

Summary of attitudes	Usually	Sometimes	Rarely	Never
Able to work with other pupils				
Cooperates with staff				
Shows qualities of leadership				
Reliable				
Shows initiative				
Maintains effort				
Willingly tackles work set				
Participates in discussion				

Try to construct a similar profile for various aspects of ability in science and try it out. A possible first line could be:

Practical ability	Usually	Sometimes	Rarely	Never
When given oral instructions, gets on with practical work without further explanation				

The Assessment of Performance Unit (APU) was set up by the government in 1975 to monitor and provide information about general levels of performance in children and young people at school. One of the curriculum areas being looked at is science. In carrying out their task, and in order to generate test items to a clear rationale, the APU science team has produced a framework of categories of scientific activity which is given in Table 13. While this framework is *not* intended to prescribe the science activities which should be undertaken in schools it does provide an interesting checklist.

TABLE 13: APU FRAMEWORK OF CATEGORIES AND SUB-CATEGORIES FOR SCIENCE

Main categories	Sub-categories	4	3	2	1
1 Using symbolic representations *(written tests)*	(a) Reading information from graphs, tables and charts (b) Expressing information as graphs, tables and charts (c) Using scientific symbols and conventions				
2 Using apparatus and measuring instruments *(practical tests)*	(a) Using measuring instruments (b) Estimating quantities (c) Following instructions for practical work				
3 Using observation *(practical tests)*	(a) Using a branching key (b) Observing similarities and differences (c) Interpreting observations				
4 Interpretation and application *(written tests)*	(4a, b and c are *not* dependent on taught science) (a) Describing and using patterns in information (b) Judging the applicability of a given generalisation (c) Distinguishing degrees of inference (4d and e are dependent on taught science) (d) Making sense of information using science concepts (e) Generating alternative hypotheses				
5 Design of investigations *(written tests)*	(a) Identifying or proposing testable statements (b) Assessing experimental procedures (c) Devising and describing investigations				
6 Performance of investigations *(practical tests)*					

Further details of the categories can be found in, for example, chapter 6 of the APU *Science in Schools, Age 13, Report No. 1.*

Activity 23:
Learning lessons from assessment procedures

1 Compare your experience of the types of assessment used in schools with the sub-categories listed by the APU. How frequently do activities of each type appear in the assessment procedures? (4 very frequently, 3 frequently, 2 occasionally, 1 rarely or never)

2 Look at the account of pupils' performances in the APU Science Reports for Teachers nos 1 and 3 (See For further study section). How do the performances described there compare with those of the children you teach in school?

Activity 24:
Understanding the way examination objectives are used

This activity is best undertaken in a group discussion.

Choose an examination for which you have taught pupils. Draw a suitable grid with question numbers on one axis and the stated examination objectives on the other. Go through a set of papers from a recent examination, one question at a time, and allocate marks to the appropriate objectives. This is easier if sub-divisions of marks within a question are given on the paper, but if they are not, create your own. Find the totals for each objective and hence the percentage of marks allocated to each. Compare this with any intentions stated on the syllabus, and comment. (A report of an exercise of this kind carried out by experienced science teachers on some 16+ examination papers is given in *Education in Science*, June and September 1982.)

For further study

Assessment of Performance Unit, Science Reports for Teachers
    1 *Science at Age 11*, HMSO, 1983
    2 *Science Assessment Framework, Age 13 and 15*, HMSO, 1984
    3 *Science at Age 13*, HMSO, 1984
    4 *Science Assessment Framework, Age 11*, HMSO, 1984
    (Other titles are in preparation)
Macintosh, H.G. and Hale, D.E., *Assessment and the Secondary School Teacher*, Routledge and Kegan Paul, 1976
Tittle, C.K. and Miller, K.M., *Assessing Attainment*, Independent Assessment and Research Centre, 1976

**Topic E
THE SCIENCE
DEPARTMENT**

The prime responsibility of a science department is to give all the pupils in the school the best science curriculum possible with the resources available. The most important resource is the *time* of the people concerned, particularly teachers and technicians, because of both its cost and its value. There are also other resources which must be used as effectively as possible, particularly: money, accommodation, equipment and materials. One of the reasons why a timetable assumes such importance in a school is that it is the basic instrument linking all these resources together.

In order to facilitate the activities related to this prime responsibility various other processes take place:

- there is a hierarchy down which jobs are delegated
- communications occur
- meetings are held
- decisions are made and acted on
- liaison takes place within and outside the department.

Problems often arise when these secondary activities are not sufficiently well developed or are inappropriate for the circumstances. Reflection on some aspects of your experience in a school science department may help you to see departmental activities in a clearer perspective, to contribute more effectively to the operation of a department and suggest features to look for when you change posts. Activity 25 gives some issues to explore.

A word of warning
Hull and Adams (1981), (see **For Further Study**) point out that if a department is to examine itself in order to improve its operation it is important that it is *the department as a whole* which is taking a critical and analytical look at itself. It is in this light that the questions which follow should be interpreted. It should not be thought that there are simple answers to any of them; to assume that is to miss the whole point. In particular, it would be inappropriate for a junior teacher or student to present his or her answers to a department.

**Activity 25:
Reflecting on some aspects
of science department
organisation and
management**

Review your experience of your own science department using the questions which follow. Discuss your thoughts with your colleagues.

1 How is the science department regarded in the school as a whole? (e.g. well-integrated, rather isolationist?)

2 Are there any major changes being planned or taking place in the department? How have these been received in the school as whole, and in the department?

3 Comment on the quality of communication in the department generally. What are the good features? Are there any problems and if so how do you think they might be solved?

4 Formal communication in a department can be made easier if there are papers to which reference can be made. Which of the following exist in the department? Comment on their usefulness. Is there additional documentation which is or could be useful?

Item	Does it Exist?	Comment
Description of department organisation		
Job descriptions for the staff		
Statement of curriculum aims or policy		
Syllabus for each course		
Scheme of work for each course		
Catalogue of apparatus, materials, books, etc. indicating where they are stored		
Regulations on safety in laboratories		
Safety file		
Policy on pupil discipline		

Policy on: homework
  : marking
  : tests
  : examinations		

Notes on keeping pupil records		
Notes on reporting to parents		

5 Comment on the following aspects of meetings in the department.

Aspect	Comment
Frequency	
When held	
Productivity	
What used for	
Advance papers used	
Minutes taken and used	
Quality of discussion	
General level of satisfaction with meetings	

6 The way in which decisions are taken in a department will probably vary depending on the school, the people involved, the type of decision and many other factors. A simple way of defining points on a spectrum of styles is as follows.

TELL   person responsible announces decision

SELL   person responsible knows what he/she wants but realises the need to sell the idea to the rest

CONSULT person responsible consults other staff but retains the right to make the decision

SHARE   within defined limits the person responsible shares the decision-making with others and does not retain a right of veto

Think about two decisions made in the department recently. How were the decisions made? Where would they come on the above spectrum? Was the appropriate style of decision-making used in each case?

7 What is the structure of the department in terms of allocation of responsibilities? How does this work with regard to the supervision of inexperienced or student teachers? How does it work more generally? For each course on which you teach is it clear to you where the responsibility lies for the following? Fill in the table and comment on any gaps which occur.

	COURSE	COURSE	COURSE	COURSE
Day-to-day running				
Team leadership				
Short-term planning				
Liaison with technicians				
Availability of apparatus, books, etc.				
Long-term planning				
Modifications to or development of the course				
Choice of exam syllabus (if applicable)				

8 Consider the way in which the apparatus is stored and distributed. Is it appropriate for the courses offered? How do you know where things are? Can you find items easily? Do you know what apparatus is available for a given topic? Is there a booking system for apparatus and is it effective?

9 What system is used for
 (i) the science department to obtain its allocation of money?
(ii) this money to be distributed within the science department?
Are these systems effective, do you think? Comment on any difficulties.

10 What liaison is there between the science department and the schools which pupils attend before they come, or go to after they leave? Comment on this situation.

For Further Study

The operation of a science department is considered in some detail in Hull, R.A. and Adams, H.B., *Decisions in the Science Department: Organisation and Curriculum*, ASE, 1981.

CONCLUSION

In December 1982 *The Times Educational Supplement* provided a feature article about the work of the Department of Education and Science concerning science education. It started like this:

> **A sense of science**. The first national survey of the grasp 15-year-olds have of science is published this week by the Government's Assessment of Performance Unit. Rosalind Driver outlines the results, which suggest that more pupils could learn to think and work scientifically if the burden of science facts was reduced.
>
> (*TES* 17.12.82)

Like all the books in this series, and those in the DES Teacher Education Project's Focus series from which they sprang, this small volume has concentrated not on *what* pupils learn, but on *how* pupils learn and *how* teachers teach.

Our hope is, that by making teachers more self-conscious about their own classroom performance, we will have taken them some steps along the road to improving their pupils' ability to think scientifically. The user can revisit this book on many occasions to review personal progress; and can pursue the various topics covered by consulting the reading list which follows.

FURTHER READING

Archenhold, W.F., Jenkins, E.W. and Wood-Robinson, C., *School Science Laboratories, a Handbook of Design, Management and Organisation*, Murray, 1978

Assessment of Performance Unit, Science Reports for Teachers, DES, 1983 onwards

Association for Science Education, *Rethinking Science*, ASE, 1984

Carré, C., *Language, Teaching and Learning: Science*, Ward Lock Educational, 1981

Creedy, J., *Laboratory Manual for Schools and Colleges*, Heinemann Educational, 1977

Dallas, D., *Teaching Biology Today*, Hutchinson, 1980

Daniels, D.J., *New Movements in the Study and Teaching of Chemistry*, Temple Smith, 1975

Davies, F. and Green, T., *Reading for Learning in Science*, Oliver and Boyd for the Schools Council, 1984

Dowdeswell, W.H., *Teaching and Learning Biology*, Heinemann Educational, 1981

Driver, R., *The Pupil as Scientist?*, Open University Press, 1983

Everett, K. and Jenkins, E.W., *A Safety Handbook for Science Teachers*, Murray, 1976

Foster, D., *Resource-based Learning in Science*, ASE (Study series no. 14), 1979

Green, E.L., *Towards Independent Learning in Science*, Hart-Davis Educational, 1976

Hull, R.A. and Adams, H.B., *Decisions in the Science Department: Organisation and Curriculum*, ASE, 1981

Hurd, P.D., *New Directions in Teaching Secondary School Science*, Rand McNally, Chicago, 1970

Ingle, R. and Jennings, A., *Science in Schools: Which Way Now?*, University of London Institute of Education, 1981

Kelly, P.J. and Wray, J.D., *The Educational Use of Living Organisms – a Source Book*, Hodder and Stoughton, 1975

Lewis, J.L., *Teaching School Physics: a Unesco Source Book*, Penguin, 1972

Lillis, K.M. and West, R.W., *Issues in Science Education: A Bibliographic Survey*, Association for Science Education, 1984

Science Teacher Education Project; a number of books on science teaching, including *The Art of the Science Teacher*, *Readings in Science Education*, *Activities and Experiences*, *Theory into Practice: Meadowbank School*, *Innovation in Teacher Education*, *Through the Eyes of the Pupil*, *Film Review*, Mcgraw-Hill, 1974

Shayer, M. and Adey, P., *Towards a Science of Science Teaching*, Heinemann Educational, 1981

Solomon, J., *Teaching Children in the Laboratory*, Croom Helm, 1980

Techniques for Assessment of Practical Skills in Foundation Science materials, Heinemann, 1983

Waring, M., *Social Pressures and Curriculum Innovation*, Methuen, 1979